Understanding Schemas and Emotion
in Early Childhood

ABOUT THE AUTHOR

Dr Cath Arnold, currently working as an Early Childhood Consultant, worked for over 30 years in private and public sector provision. Cath has written two previous books about her grandchildren's early development and learning and is very committed to working alongside parents to understand young children's development and learning.

THE PEN GREEN TEAM

The Pen Green Team are a team of researchers and nursery workers who all collaborated in a study of children's Well-being and Resilience from 2001–2004. This book tells **a very small** part of the story of that study and is just one of the outcomes of the four year study. The study was partly funded by the Esmee Fairbairn Charitable Trust and further funded and fully supported by the Pen Green Research, Development and Training Base, Corby, Northants, a self-financing organisation. As lead author, I am very grateful to the funders for the opportunity to work in such an innovative and intimate way with a small number of families.

The full time researchers involved were: Dr Margy Whalley, Dr Cath Arnold, Marcus Dennison, Colette Tait, Eddie McKinnon and Robert Orr. In addition, Dr Natasha Charlwood carried out Adult Attachment Interviews with parents at the start of the study and made links between parents' attachment experiences and children's social and emotional well-being, which was subsequently reported in an EECERA journal article (Charlwood and Steele, 2004). Maggie Haggerty (Senior Lecturer in Early Childhood Education at Victoria University of Wellington, New Zealand) worked as part of the team for the first year of the study and contributed hugely to our thinking about young children's well-being.

The full time nursery workers involved were: the late Katey Mairs (Deputy Head of the Pen Green Centre), Angela Prodger (Head of Nursery), Annette Cummings, Louise King, Michele McCabe, Michelle McGinn, Denise Hammond, Margaret Myles and Tracy Coull.

All of these workers along with the parents involved made major contributions to the study reported in the unpublished report available at the Pen Green Centre, 'A Research and Development Project to Promote Well-being and Resilience in Young Children' (Pen Green Team, 2004). All workers and researchers involved, engaged in deep and challenging dialogue with parents about their children's well-being and resilience. The learning from the study has become embedded in practice at the Pen Green Centre and has informed our engagement with children and families in many many ways.

Understanding Schemas and Emotion in Early Childhood

CATH ARNOLD
and the Pen Green Team

Los Angeles | London | New Delhi
Singapore | Washington DC

Reprinted 2010

SAGE Publications Ltd
1 Oliver's Yard
55 City Road
London EC1Y 1SP

SAGE Publications Inc.
2455 Teller Road
Thousand Oaks, California 91320

SAGE Publications India Pvt Ltd
B 1/I 1 Mohan Cooperative Industrial Area
Mathura Road
New Delhi 110 044

SAGE Publications Asia-Pacific Pte Ltd
33 Pekin Street #02–01
Far East Square
Singapore 048763

Library of Congress Control Number: 2009931135
British Library Cataloguing in Publication data

A catalogue record for this book is available from the British Library

ISBN 978-1-84920-165-0
ISBN 978-1-84920-166-7 (pbk)

Typeset by Dorwyn, Wells, Somerset
Printed in Great Britain by the MPG Books Group
Printed on paper from sustainable resources

Mixed Sources
Product group from well-managed forests and other controlled sources
www.fsc.org Cert no. SA-COC-1565
© 1996 Forest Stewardship Council
FSC

Contents

Acknowledgements

There are many people to thank for their contributions to this work; first, the children and families who were involved and have been a great support throughout and who, we hope, gained from their experiences; secondly, the nursery workers, who were always generous in sharing their ideas and time with us; thirdly, the research team, particularly Margy Whalley, who initiated the idea of studying young children's well-being and resilience alongside their families and workers, and led, supported and helped sustain our interest and involvement over the four years; fourthly, our many 'critical friends', Professor Chris Pascal, Professor Julia Formosinho, Chris Athey, Professor Colwyn Trevarthen, Professor Colin Fletcher, Dr John Woolley, Dr Janet Shaw and many, many others, who popped into the Research Base during this time.

Personally, I'd like to thank my family for supporting me with technical support and meals (Terry), proofreading and questions (Colette and Eloise), interest (Paul) and inspiration (Georgia and Harry). I would like to give a special thanks to Chris Athey, who has been my guru and friend for many years now and who constantly keeps me on my toes with regard to evidence-based research and constructivism, among other things.

The author and publishers would like to thank the following for permission:

Introduction:

Isaacs, S. (1952) 'The Nature and Function of Phantasy' in Riviere, J. *Developments in Psychoanalysis*, Hogarth Press, London.

Chapter 5:

From: Arnold, C. (2009) 'Understanding 'Together and Apart': a case study of Edward's explorations at nursery', *Early Years Journal*, vol. 29, no. 2, pp. 119–30. Reprinted by permission of the publisher (Taylor & Francis Group, www.informaworld.com).

Chapter 6:

From: Arnold, C. (2009) 'A case study showing how one young child represented issues concerned with attachment and separation in her spontaneous explorations', EECERA Journal, vol. 17, no.1, pp. 147–62. Reprinted by permission of the publisher (Taylor & Francis Group, www.informaworld.com).

Conventions Used in this Book

- Schemas are underlined and refer to the 'form' of actions and thinking.

- Observations are italicised, as are quotes at the beginning of chapters.

- The use of 'we' and 'I' – the 'Well-being and Resilience' study carried out at the Pen Green Centre from 2000 to 2004 involved a team of researchers, workers, parents and children all collaborating together. Much of this book is expressed as 'we' to reflect the investigation carried out by all of the people involved. Aspects of the study that affected only me, my personal experiences and my personal learning, for example in Chapter 9, are expressed as 'I'.

- I use the concept of 'emotion' rather than the concept of 'feeling' to describe what is observable in the body movement, actions and language of each child. 'Feeling' seems to be the private unobservable aspect of emotion (Damasio, 1999).

It is through feelings, which are inwardly directed and private, that emotions, which are outwardly directed and public, begin their impact on the mind; but the full and lasting impact of feelings requires consciousness, because only along with the advent of a sense of self do feelings become known to the person having them. (Damasio, 1999, p. 36)

Outline of this Book

This book is designed so that chapters can be read independently of each other. A similar structure is used throughout: we begin each chapter with an opening summary, then 'Introduction and context', followed by 'Observations, discussions and interpretations'. We then try to address the 'So what?' question and end with schemas mentioned and suggested further reading.

Chapter 1 is about engaging in Child Study and also presents ideas for making useful observations and analysing them.

In Chapter 2, we meet Ewan, who demonstrated his need for a ritualised separation. We consider how that need manifested itself in his play and contributed to his coping with short separations from his parents.

In Chapter 3, we introduce John, who explored <u>lines</u> and <u>connecting</u> extensively in his effort to gain control of his world. John also came to something of an understanding of separations through his play.

Chapter 4 describes Caitlin's explorations of <u>containing</u>, <u>enveloping</u> and <u>transporting</u> and how she drew on these patterns of action when her security was under threat.

Chapter 5 shows Edward's explorations of 'together' and 'apart' through his repeated actions of <u>connecting</u> and <u>disconnecting</u>. The chapter also presents observations of Edward's investigation of going from the '<u>vertical</u>' position to the '<u>horizontal</u>' position.

Chapter 6 depicts Sam's explorations of <u>enveloping</u>, <u>containing</u> and <u>seriation</u> at a time when she was trying to understand 'presence' and 'absence' and issues around power.

Chapter 7 describes Susan's explorations of <u>containing</u>, <u>enveloping</u> and <u>going through a boundary</u> to understand separation and loss.

Chapter 8 focuses on the death of Cara's Great Uncle and her explorations of death and loss.

Shaw found that when she paid attention to emotions in others, she was surprised by the emotions evoked in her and that at times she 'was overwhelmed by the pain' of others (1991, p. 267).

In Chapter 9, I describe my growing awareness of my own responses to emotions and emotional events.

Chapter 10 draws together some conclusions and proposes a new concept to explain how human beings use repeated patterns to understand emotional experiences and moral issues.

Foreword

By Margy Whalley

Only an education which takes very seriously the child's view of things can change the world for the better ... The power relationships between adults and children are all wrong and they must be changed, so adults can no longer be convinced that they are right to arrange the life and world of the child as they see best without consulting the child's feelings ... Janusz Korczak

Pen Green Centre for Children and their Families opened in 1983 and our central concern was always that children using the services should feel strong, able to question and challenge, able to make good choices and that they should be emotionally resilient. As early childhood educators we were constructivists trying hard to understand and support children's passion for learning. We were hungry to develop what Chris Athey describes as a more conscious and articulated pedagogy. As a staff group we owe a huge debt of gratitude to the giants whose shoulders we stand on. We have been fortunate indeed to work directly over many years with Chris Athey and with Tina Bruce. We have also been able to develop our thinking through the practical application of Chris Athey's Schema theory in the work of Janet Shaw and Patrick Easen. Cath Arnold's study builds on this strong tradition of thinking deeply about children's cognitive concerns.

Initially, in early 1988, when Chris Athey first attended a Pen Green staff and parent training session and shared her ideas with us, staff were challenged and taken a long way out of their comfort zone. It became clear during the session that it was the parents who were better able to listen and apply their new understandings. Parents could draw on their own intimate observations of their children at home, and eagerly contributed to the debate. They were keen to share knowledge about how their children were learning at home and confidently describe the schemas they had spotted. One mother shared with us how her daughter repeatedly put toothpaste all around the outside edge of her mug. Another told us how her son was hanging things from trees in the garden and repeatedly using string to tie up the house, attaching string to door handles and banisters. Some of this play really disturbed the mother who associated what he was doing with the macabre – making nooses and hanging. She was very reassured to find out that he had a 'Connecting Schema'.

Staff struggled at first with what seemed like a new pedagogical language. They were accustomed to robustly observing children in the Susan Isaacs tradition but needed to become much stronger theoretically. Assessment frameworks had to change and Possible Lines of Direction Plans (PLODs) were developed that documented the learning journey of each child. For the first time nursery planning sessions included exhaustive theoretical discussions about the laws of physics. Parents and staff became equally committed to celebrating the children's achievements and helping them to be all that they could be.

Twenty-one years later staff and parents still dialogue, debate and work collaboratively to support the children's learning and development at Pen Green. Many of the parents who attended that first session with Chris Athey went on to participate in our Parents Involvement In Children's Learning programme and Cath made a major contribution developing this work. Parents attended study groups, received accreditation, engaged in their own studies and professional development and continue to this day to support their children's studies.

Pen Green has always been a place where children were able to express strong emotions. As a staff group we have always wanted to respect children's right to express their anger and their sadness. Our deepening understanding of Schema theory helped us to extend and support their thinking and at the same time we wanted to support them in expressing, understanding and dealing with their feelings. In this seminal book Cath Arnold plots the development of our shared understanding about how children's emotional needs and cognitive concerns can best be supported. She describes how a deep understanding of children's schemas can illuminate how children are making sense of their often challenging worlds. Cath's wonderfully rich case studies of Ewan, John, Caitlin, Edward, Sam, Susan and Cara are all drawn from data gathered by the Pen Green Research Base during the period 2000–2004. These case studies powerfully illustrate how children respond to the stressors in their lives. Cath skilfully examines how children are affected by grief and loss, estrangement, parental depression and parental lack of responsiveness. She explores children's need to feel powerful, authoritative and leaderful within the nursery setting when they are dealing with complexity and adversity at home. She shows how challenge and adversity – what Rutter describes as steeling experiences – can actually increase children's resilience and sense of self efficacy. Each of the case studies demonstrates the vitally important role of their key worker in the nursery.

In her concluding chapters Cath acknowledges the importance of technical supervision for staff working at the emotional 'coal face'. If staff are to take account of children's feelings, if staff are to effectively advocate on behalf of children and sustain parents in their critical role as the child's first educator and most effective advocate, the staff must also feel contained through the supervisory process.

Cath is unrelenting in her commitment to developing nursery staff as practioner researchers. She is concerned that they should be capable of challenging their own practice and at the same time able to engage with theory. Cath takes us on a journey through the writings of Piaget, Vygotsky, Freud, Bowlby and Winnicott to our contempories Trevarthen, Kraemer and Steele, academic colleagues who have all worked directly with staff in the Pen Green nursery and research base. Cath has courageously identified her own 'ghosts' which have impacted on her practice as a pedagogue and parent. Her challenge to all of us working with children and their families is to reflect deeply on our own experiences and develop appropriate support within our settings so that we can confront our own issues. Then and only then will we be emotionally available, able to effectively engage with children and their families as companions in their learning.

Introduction

A schema is a mode of reactions susceptible of reproducing themselves and susceptible above all of being generalized. (Piaget, 1962, p. 95)

Schemas are patterns of repeatable actions that lead to early categories and then to logical classifications. (Athey, 2007, p. 49)

Recognition of the child's schemas appears to give the parent and teacher access to the child's emotional experience in addition to her intellectual development. (Shaw, 1991, p. 6)

This chapter introduces:

- The context in which a study of young children's schemas and emotional experiences took place

- A brief examination of the theory used to illuminate children's actions

- A critical incident that prompted a closer look at schemas and emotion and resulted in some new learning about how young children use schemas

- A plan of this book

We begin this account with three quotes: the first from Piaget, who wrote extensively about schemas and offered a theory to explain young children's development and learning. Piaget and Inhelder proposed that human beings learn through repeatedly acting on objects and materials within the environment. They identified many of these early actions, 'like putting things next to one another (proximity) or in series (order), actions of enclosing, of tightening or loosening, changing viewpoints, cutting, rotating, folding or unfolding, enlarging and reducing and so on' (Piaget and Inhelder, 1956, p. 453).

Piaget believed that as human beings, we build up working theories through repeating our actions. We 'assimilate' new content into our current models or structures (he meant schemas) and sometimes have to 'accommodate' our actions and knowledge when something unexpected happens (Piaget, 1950/2001, p. 8). This is when we might adapt our actions and learn new patterns or adapt our actions to continue exploring a pattern we are using.

The second quote is from Chris Athey, whose seminal text has made Piaget's work accessible to many teachers and Early Childhood workers. She has also applied Piaget's theories to children aged 2–5 years (Athey, 2007). Her research and positive view of young children's cognitive development, hand in hand with recent research on the brain, has changed our view of young children. Unlike Piaget, who seemed to focus on a deficit view of children (signified by what they had not achieved or learned so far), Athey saw children as able and competent, actively seeking new content to assimilate into current structures (or schemas).

The third quote is from Janet Shaw, less well known, but the first person to pursue the link between schemas and emotion in early childhood. Shaw was a home-visiting teacher in the North of England, who on visits to vulnerable families, shared ideas with parents about their children's repeated actions or schemas (Shaw, 1991, p. 110).

Shaw put forward this idea of a connection between schemas and emotions, an idea that had fascinated parents and Early Childhood workers at the Pen Green Centre for a number of years. Many parents and workers, who have closely observed young children and been able to spot their repeated patterns of action, have wondered what motivates children to use particular patterns over time. There seems to be no strict hierarchy in the order in which schemas emerge, although it is well established that children always build on their own earlier learning (Athey, 2007; Meade and Cubey, 2008; Nutbrown, 2006). Shaw also ventured into a field new to her, that of psychoanalytic theory, just as we have done in this recent study of young children and schemas.

THE INFLUENCE OF VYGOTSKY

Although Piaget and his followers have influenced our thinking about young children and their development and learning, we have also been influenced by Vygotsky, whose main focus was on the role of other people in children's development. Vygotsky's theory was that,

> Every function in the child's cultural development appears twice: first on the social level, and later on the individual level; first, between people (interpsychological) and then inside the child (intrapsychological). This

applies equally to voluntary attention, to logical memory, and to the formation of concepts. (1978, p. 57)

Each child's world begins with the family context and events that occur within that context. In this book we try to make links between observed and identified patterns or schemas and each child's sociocultural context at the time. We believe that schemas are 'universals' but that the cultural context, including emotional aspects, seem to flesh out particular behaviours at certain times.

THIS BOOK

This book is about 'a subject whose time has come' (Whalley, 2009). We are not about to abandon any of our rigour or learning about cognitive development in favour of a 'soft' or cosy approach to thinking about emotions. We are trying to demonstrate some possible motives for children's actions, as well as trying to figure out how cognition in action can assist young children in processing and coming to understand very real emotional events in their lives.

THE WIDER CONTEXT

The children we introduce to you in this book were part of a bigger study of young children's well-being and resilience, which took place at the Pen Green Nursery from 2000 to 2004 (Pen Green Team, 2004).

The Pen Green Centre for Under Fives and Their Families was set up in 1983 in what was considered a disadvantaged area of the Midlands. The centre provided services for the local community which responded to local need and grew gradually from the bottom up. Today, the centre provides:

Early years education

Extended hours, extended year provision to support families

Inclusive, flexible education with care for children in need and children with special educational needs

Adult community education and family support services

Voluntary work and community regeneration

Training and support for early years practitioners

Research and development. (Whalley, 2007, p. 5)

The Pen Green Research Base was set up in 1996 in order to debate 'teaching and learning and curriculum issues with parents' and more widely in the early years community (Whalley, 2007, p. 9). The first major research study, funded by the Esmee Fairbairn Trust, was on 'Involving parents in their children's learning' and was documented in the book of that name by Margy Whalley and the Pen Green Team. The study of young children's well-being and resilience built on our earlier learning and that, too, was partly funded by the Esmee Fairbairn Trust.

THE CONTEXT OF THIS STUDY

As a research team, we worked in partnership with the children, their parents and workers. Fifty-eight children were studied over a period of four years. We filmed the children in nursery and some parents also filmed their children at home. Then we met with the parents, workers and sometimes children too, to discuss and interpret what we saw on film. This technique was something we had tried out before (Whalley, 2007, p. 70). The parents and children brought information from home and about family events and we brought some child development theory to the discussions. Together, we formed what Easen et al. have described as a 'developmental partnership' in order to benefit the children and also to further knowledge in the field (Easen et al., 1992, p. 287).

OUR KNOWLEDGE BASE

Since the late 1980s, as workers and parents at the Pen Green Centre, we had been identifying children's schemas in order to support the children's cognitive concerns and explorations, both at nursery and at home. We had considerably changed our environment and routines at nursery in order to maximise the opportunities for children to explore their current concerns and to become deeply 'involved' in play (Laevers, 1997, p. 20).

As a result of our work with schemas, many parents found themselves providing resources such as, for example, string and sellotape for their children to connect as Christmas gifts, rather than more expensive manufactured toys. We were supported in this ongoing study of children's schemas by Tina Bruce and Chris Athey over a number of years. Defining schemas and sharing that information with parents, was both a challenge and a joy. We sometimes struggled to explain what we meant by 'schemas' to the parents, but viewing video vignettes of their children helped to communicate this idea of 'repeated actions' (the movement aspect) and resulting 'configurations' (the shape). Matthews drew on brain research to conclude that, as human beings, we seek information about the 'shape' and 'movement' of objects and events (Matthews, 2003, p. 23).

◀ Offering clay for children to work in three dimensions

Maple blocks ▶

◀ Writing and communication

Books at children's level ▶

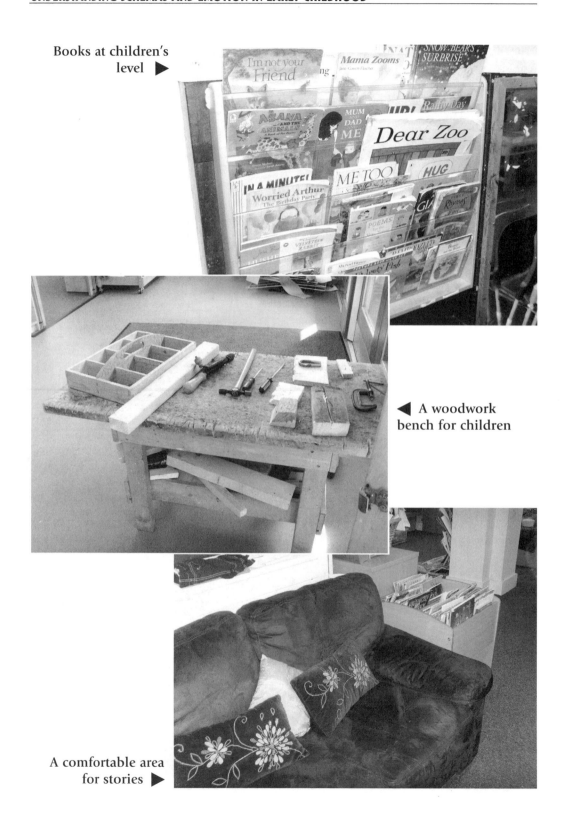

◀ A woodwork bench for children

A comfortable area for stories ▶

◀ The outdoor area and bridge that connects the nursery gardens

Resources for sand and water play ▶

◀ A sunken sandpit in the snug

Water run in the
discovery area ▶

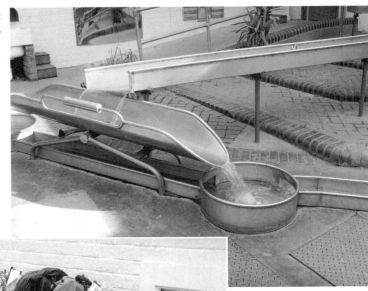

◀ Dressing up in the
discovery area

Out of doors at the
Pen Green Nursery ▶

For example, when Georgia was interested in <u>rotation</u>, she not only explored that movement in action with her whole body and with objects, she also seemed sensitive to round shapes and created many pages of curved 'writing'. Around the same time she became interested in making friendship bracelets and in playing 'Ring-a-roses' and 'Farmer's in the den' (Arnold, 1999, p. 43). Her parents jotted their observations of her actions in a diary and could see a clear pattern across time. Most parents we engaged with could spot their children exploring one or more repeated patterns of action.

When embarking on a study of young children's well-being and resilience, we began to study 'attachment theory' and other psychoanalytic theories. Bowlby defined 'attachment' as 'seeking and maintaining proximity to another individual' (Bowlby, 1997, p. 195). Bowlby observed that young animals and humans very quickly (within weeks of birth) 'recognised their primary caregiver' and that this 'preference was extremely strong and persistent' (p. 196). He noticed specific behaviours that indicated how secure children were in their attachment to their parents and caregivers. This theory was particularly relevant to us, as parents and workers, seeking to understand what builds resilience and helps children to feel secure.

We were aware of the huge body of work on infant observation, from a psychoanalytic standpoint but were unclear as to whether we could relate the theory to all children and families using mainstream services (Adamo, 2008; Fonagy, 2001; Miller et al., 1989; Stern, 1998).

A PERSONAL CRITICAL INCIDENT

Some four years after filming Harry (my grandson) as a 3-year-old, <u>connecting</u> with string, I showed a video sequence of Harry to a group of MA students. The session was about Piaget's work and a colleague was going to talk about the work of Winnicott afterwards. My daughter (Harry's mother) had joined the group because of an interest in the theory, although she was not studying at the time. I can only describe myself as 'frozen' emotionally when my colleague, in his talk about Winnicott, referred back to the video sequence I had just shown of Harry and introduced the group to a paper written by Winnicott in 1960 on the subject of 'String: a technique of communication' (Winnicott, 1990, p. 153). In the paper, Winnicott referred to a boy, aged seven, who was 'obsessed with everything to do with string' (p. 154). As well as 'connecting' bits of furniture together with string (in a similar way to what we had just observed Harry doing on film) the boy's parents were worried that 'He had recently tied a string around his sister's neck'. This link between 'connecting' with string and this boy's anxiety seemed rather extreme and created an 'emotional jar' for me and for others in the group. However, on reflection, I could begin to see that there could be a link between Harry's strong desire to 'connect' and his emotional world at that time.

Harry's parents separated when he was just 3 years old. His mother moved to a house two streets away and he and his sister began spending Monday to Friday living in their mum's house and Saturday to Monday living in their dad's house (Arnold, 2003, p. 60). Despite Harry's distress at the time, I had not thought of his repeated pattern of <u>connecting</u> as anything other than a cognitive act.

When my colleague made this connection, I felt the 'emotional jar' more keenly than most other people in the room (apart from Harry's mother). I had intimate knowledge of Harry's home circumstances and observations of how he had coped with the separation of his parents. I had been reluctant to accept the emotional significance of many of the observations we had made of Harry and had chosen to focus only on his cognitive gains as that was less painful for me and for us as a family.

OTHER RELATED OBSERVATIONS

As researchers, we began to recognise other links in the literature, for example, in Susan Isaacs work where she described a 2-year-old boy, distressed on his second day at nursery.

> He stood by the observer, holding her hand and at first sobbing, occasionally asking 'Mummy coming, Mummy coming?' A tower of small bricks was placed on a chair near him. At first he ignored the bricks, then when another child had a box of bricks nearby, he quickly carried to this box all but two of the bricks on the chair. The remaining two, a small cube and a large triangular brick, he placed together on the chair, touching each other, in a position similar to that of himself and the observer who was seated beside him. He then came back and again held the adult's hand. Now he was able to stop crying, and seemed much calmer. (Isaacs, 1952, p. 115)

Isaacs explained that 'here we see a child comforting himself and overcoming feelings of loss and terror by a symbolic act with two material objects' (Isaacs, 1952, p. 116). The boy seemed to represent his wish to be reunited with his mother but also seemed to be comforted by placing two objects in close proximity to each other.

Athey, herself, described Lois, who was interested in exploring a <u>containing</u> and <u>enveloping</u> schema (2007, p. 143). When Lois 'drew her brother and covered the whole drawing and said "I've covered him up with a blanket" and added "And I'll put the cot in a cupboard [pause] and I'll put the cupboard in a cave"', Athey chose not to use a Freudian framework to analyse Lois's actions. Athey wanted to stay with the non-deficit or positive view (as she saw it) of Lois's actions. We began to wonder whether having a new brother had prompted Lois's keen interest in <u>containing</u> and <u>enveloping.</u> Could Lois be exploring her emotional experience and furthering her understanding of her own feelings about having a new brother? Was she using her cognition (schemas or repeated patterns) to give form to her negative feelings about her brother?

In this book, we explore the experiences of seven children at nursery, by identifying their schematic play and making possible links with their relationships and emotional worlds. Through this research we discovered that schemas are not necessarily prompted by emotional events, but that there are close links between the exploration of particular patterns or schemas and understanding emotional events. Young children seem to use schemas or repeated patterns of action for **comfort**, to **give form to**, and to **explore and begin to understand complex life events and changes.**

Early Years Practitioners and Parents Engaging in Child Study

Michelle, one of the nursery workers, had been on a course the day before. Claudette had worked as a supply worker to 'cover' Michelle's group. On her return, one of the children, James, made the following comment to Michelle: 'You weren't here last night and Claudette covered you all up'.

(Here James seemed to use his concrete experiences of 'covering' or <u>enveloping</u> to understand the fact that Michelle was not at nursery and that Claudette was there. Even the adults used the metaphor of 'covering' to express the concept that when one worker is not there carrying out her role, another replaces her.)

This chapter introduces:

- The important tradition of Child Study in Early Childhood

- How we approached children and families to carry out this study of children

- Carrying out observations and the different tools we have used

- Interpretation of observations using schema theory and psychoanalytic theory

INTRODUCTION AND CONTEXT

We have a strong tradition both in the UK and in the field of Early Education, of making observations of young children engaged in play and conversation in order to understand their development and learning (Bartholomew and Bruce,

1993; Isaacs, 1930/1966, 1933; Piaget, 1951). Within education and care settings, we observe in order to make plans for each child's learning. At the Pen Green Centre and other early childhood settings, parents have been central to making observations of their own children as they know their own children best (Whalley, 1997, 2007). When we observe, we are trying to understand what each child is trying to learn about, so that we can tune in to and support their cognitive and emotional concerns. Workers, who are with children every day, can get to know children and families well but they also depend on parents supplying information from home, including who are important adults and other children to their child. Knowing about where families go and who they meet up with during the week can enable Early Years Educators to have genuine and meaningful conversations with children when their parents are not around.

LOOKING BACK AT OUR TRADITION OF CHILD STUDY

OBSERVATION TECHNIQUES FROM EARLY CHILDHOOD EDUCATION

Susan Isaacs' accounts of young children's development and learning in the Malting House School, Cambridge, early in the twentieth century, has provided a way of recording and interpreting children's spontaneous actions, that is still relevant in the twenty-first century. Isaacs took cognition and emotions into account and produced two books on the children's development, one focusing on 'intellectual growth' and the second focusing on the children's 'social development' (1930/1966, 1933). The important learning for us today, was that Susan Isaacs did not compartmentalise these aspects. She used the rich, detailed observations of children, gathered over time, to understand their intellectual **and** emotional development. She presented the observations first and then made her analysis and interpretations. These first-hand observations can be treated as raw data, even today, nearly 80 years later.

Here is an example from Isaacs' writing showing the determination and resourcefulness of one child:

17.10.24 (Date) The children had been carrying water out into the garden in cans and jugs, and as there were some damp feet, Mrs. I. Said 'No more today'. Tommy (2;8) (age) was doleful when Mrs. I. would not let him take any more, and passing back through the school room, he saw the vases on the tables, full of flowers. Without saying anything, he put down his can on the floor, and took each of the four vases in turn, lifting the flowers out, pouring the water into his can, and putting the flowers back, and the vase back on the table. He then walked out into the garden smiling, and saying to the others, 'Tommy has some water now!' (Isaacs, 1930, p. 120)

We can draw a great deal from this one observation. **Practically**, Isaacs states the exact date, the age of the child being observed and enough detail for the reader to grasp what happened without getting lost in too much detail. Many workers trained in the UK have been well trained to observe and to record detail, but that detail can be irrelevant and not critical to what happened; for example in this case, it was not important to know the grip Tommy used to carry the can.

With regard to **pedagogy**, we can deduce that there was a fair amount of freedom but that boundaries were set, that is, 'No more today'. However, there was also flexibility. Whoever observed Tommy was truly interested in what he would do next. That deep interest in children's spontaneous actions is important.

As far as Tommy's **development** is concerned, at 2 years 8 months, he seemed to be interested in <u>containing</u> and <u>transporting</u> materials. He may have been able to use his <u>containment</u> schema at thought level with regard to his understanding that vases may <u>contain</u> water (even if the water cannot be seen). We are not told whether the vases were opaque, translucent or transparent. Even if the vases were transparent, he was able to come up with a plan to transfer water from the vases into his own can, demonstrating some flexibility in thinking and problem-solving. At the least, he could see that carrying more water outside was 'functionally dependent' on him transferring or <u>transporting</u> it from one <u>container</u> into another (Athey, 2007, p. 119). He also demonstrated some satisfaction in achieving his personal goal.

A contemporary of Susan Isaacs took a similar approach to the study of young children's development in New York, early in the twentieth century. The children who attended 'The Nursery School' ranged in age from 14 months to 3 years. Harriett Johnson's account also contains photos, showing how very rich the experiences offered to the children were (Johnson, 1972, pp. 170–1). Like Isaacs, and more recently Chris Athey, Johnson stated her beliefs clearly at the beginning of her account, 'The duty of the educator is to see that the capacities of each stage are fully realized, not that the stages succeed each other as rapidly as possible' (Johnson, 1972, p. xxxi).

Johnson gathered narrative observations to try to capture learning in action in young children. Johnson illustrated how individual children mastered skills over time, for example, using a slide or hammering nails. She followed Philip's progress, over time, in using both the indoor and outdoor slides. Here is a short excerpt from her observations. She was interested in his use of the slide and his control of his own body. The slide was high and Philip was practising going down head first on his stomach.

24 months (Philip's age) – Adult table was placed under the chute so that the children could climb and slide from the 'half-way station'. Philip was very appreciative of this arrangement which was placed for

some older children. He continued after the others had left. They had pulled up an adult chair to stand in and once he stopped there to call 'Bye, bye, bye' at least a dozen times. He also paused on top of the table to shout 'Dah,dah'. He gave every evidence of elation and joy. (Johnson, 1972, p. 175)

Philip seemed to be repeating his actions in order to master his use of the slide. Using schema theory to interpret his actions, he was exploring an oblique trajectory, feeling the angle and resulting speed. He had probably mastered sitting and sliding down, and now he was varying the position of his body in order to experience the angle and speed differently. In emotional terms, he was deliberately taking on a challenge. He 'marked' or acknowledged this challenge with the language of separation by saying 'Bye, bye, bye'. This may have simply represented his departure onto the slide. It may also have represented his departure from his earlier state of not being confident about sliding down on his stomach to practising and becoming more confident. Philip may have been echoing language used by his parents or workers in similar situations that he had subsequently internalised as a way of behaving in times of challenge or struggle. He was very pleased with himself, what Trevarthen (2003) and then Tait (2005) have called 'chuffed' with himself.

The important point about making narrative observations is that we begin by observing and can then make links with any curriculum framework. We can also use any theory as a framework to deepen our understanding of children's actions and interactions. In this book, we use schema theory and attachment theory to deepen our understanding. We could also make links with the Early Years Foundation Stage Guidance, currently used in settings in England.

AN OBSERVATION TECHNIQUE FROM THE FIELD OF PSYCHOANALYSIS

The Tavistock method of Infant Observation Training involves the observer in visiting a newborn and family weekly for two years. The observation is recorded afterwards and is presented as the material for a work discussion group. The observer is open to the feelings evoked in him/her. Rustin (1989, p. 7) describes the method: 'The practice of systematic observation of the development of infants provides the observer with an opportunity to encounter primitive emotional states in the infant and his family, and indeed in the observer's own response to this turbulent environment.'

Although this intense and time-consuming course is intended to be part of the training for child psychotherapy, Rustin (1989, p. 8) points out that 'it has also proved very valuable for professional development of other workers in a variety of roles with children'.

▨ MAKING CHILDREN'S DEVELOPMENT AND LEARNING VISIBLE

One way of making children's development and learning visible, and the focus of discussion, is through pedagogical documentation. We, at Pen Green, have learned a great deal from the Reggio Project. We have been challenged to think in different ways, acknowledging the importance of the group as well as individuals within each group. In Reggio, the workers focus on children's projects and each project is beautifully documented. A great deal of their documentation includes children's detailed drawings or photographs of sculptures or paintings, that often give insights into children's thinking and feeling. Carla Rinaldi (2006, p. 68) has written about the purposes and advantages of pedagogical documentation:

> To ensure listening and being listened to is one of the primary tasks of documentation (producing traces/documents that testify to and make visible the ways of learning of the individuals and the group) as well as to ensure that the group and each individual child have the possibility to observe themselves from an external view while they are learning …

Documentation makes revisiting and reviewing our thinking possible. Rinaldi also speaks about observation, not seen as 'an individual action' but 'a reciprocal relationship' (2006, p. 128). Rather than seeing observation as the task of one person, who tries to be objective, Rinaldi says 'Instead we have a world of multiple interacting subjects who construct reality starting from different points of view' (p. 128). She sees observing as 'not so much perceiving reality as constructing reality' (p. 128).

HOW WE APPROACHED CHILDREN AND FAMILIES TO CARRY OUT THIS STUDY

Workers and parents at the Pen Green Centre have built a tradition over 26 years of engaging in Child Study, to understand and provide exciting possibilities for children and as part of workers' own professional development. So, when we embarked on a new study, many parents using the nursery, were aware of what had gone before. Rather than attempting to be 'objective' by choosing to study children in a randomised way, we began by building on relationships with families we already knew and who were interested. Rigour does not necessarily come from being objective but from being aware of our subjective view.

As workers, we approached the parents, who we thought might be interested, individually at first. We explained what the study might involve and how the parents might engage with us in studying their children. It was important to indicate how much material we would gather and how often and where we would meet with families to discuss and interpret our nursery observations and to hear about observations made at home. As always, we were flexible about how often and where we met. In a study of 'Involving parents in their children's learning', focusing mainly on cognition, we had found meetings where parents viewed and discussed their own and each other's children's development and learning to be hugely successful. In this project both workers and families seemed more comfortable discussing emotions in smaller groups or in a one to one dialogue.

ETHICS

An important aspect of any Child Study is ethics. I have found making initial contact with anyone, who might participate in a study, and talking through with them, as individuals, what might happen, critical to any study. Although confidentiality and anonymity may be desirable, the use of photographs and video material has made it almost impossible to anonymise the people involved.

In order to gain permission for this study, I spent time with parents and with children before any filming was done. Occasionally children felt uncomfortable being filmed and usually indicated their discomfort by their actions, for example, one day one little girl avoided me by going inside a tent and closing the zip. Sometimes children were pleased to see me and would chat or tell me where they were going to play next. One child claimed me as 'her' researcher and would tell other children that I was there to film 'her' and not them.

Workers in settings where an outsider comes in to film can feel quite vulnerable (Tobin and Davidson, 1990, p. 273). Asking individually for permission in such a way that children, parents or workers can say 'No' takes quite a bit of skill and we have not always got it right. Holding in mind that we hope to share power with others and to hear their views helps to some extent. Seeking permission at each stage of a study also communicates the message that permission may be given or withheld at any point and for any reason.

CARRYING OUT OBSERVATIONS USING DIFFERENT TOOLS

Generally speaking we notice what has significance for us. Children interested in grid-like shapes might notice the net curtains, scaffolding on the way to nursery and a tartan biscuit tin on the table, all of which have a grid-like form. As adults, we might notice children exploring repeated patterns (schemas) because we have recently been discussing and articulating what those patterns might look like. We may be sensitive to certain patterns at different times.

In order to observe, we need to pay close attention, a kind of active watching and listening. When we reflect on our observations of children, we sometimes use different tools to capture the main events. These are mostly:

- pen and paper
- Dictaphone
- camera
- video recorder.

If we are using the Tavistock Method (as mentioned earlier) we would watch carefully and record (using pen and paper or a computer) as much detail as possible afterwards, paying special attention to recording our feelings, as well as what we have observed in the interactions of others.

Adopting the technique Susan Isaacs and other proponents of Child Study used, means keeping a 'running record' of actions and language, often gathered while we are engaging with the children (Bartholomew and Bruce, 1993, p. 16). In Susan Isaacs' day, that meant carrying a notebook and pen and filling in the detail afterwards. It was and is most important to record accurately any language being used by the children, as language can provide such insights into children's thinking, as we saw with James at the start of this chapter. Dictaphones can be useful for recording children's language as well as our reflections on their actions.

We became interested in processes of learning rather than outcomes of learning and we found these processes were most easily captured by taking a sequence of photos or by filming. We could communicate what we thought we had seen with a set of photos. Filming added another dimension, enabling us to view the filmed material alongside parents. Tait (2007, p. 69) noted that 'The video we watched acted as a catalyst for dialogue', when working with a parent. She went on to point out that 'It was a tool that allowed us to revisit, review and reflect on what had been filmed'. The parent Tait worked with was able to 'see things from a totally different perspective'. Somehow, using video seemed to offer parents an opportunity to be alongside workers as equals, both expressing views and coming to 'a shared understanding' (Tait, 2007, p. 60).

Trevarthen (2006) described 'emotion as the quality of movement' and because we wanted to be able to gain a deeper understanding of children's emotions, we found filming to be most effective and useful. Jordan and Henderson (1995, p. 51) pointed out that 'video taping … produces data much closer to the event itself, than other kinds of re-presentation'. Holding a camera sometimes affected children's behaviour but, if they did not object to being filmed, they soon seemed to get used to the camera. Very occasionally a child was so interested in the camera and how it worked that it was impossible to film their involvement without the aid of a second camera.

In writing up the material for this book, I have become aware of another issue around video observations. When we watch video, we pick up so much information through all of our senses, that representing the observation in the written word is quite difficult. The advantage of video is being able to revisit and review original material in all of its complexity. In revisiting observations we see more each time, and representing that detail sometimes results in loss of communication with others. Another difficulty is presenting observations without judgement initially because, as human beings, we are analysing and trying to make sense of events all of the time. Narrative observations can be so long and complicated that the reader gets lost and misses the point. In settings, there may be no reason to transcribe everything observed, as filmed material can be part of a child's record of development and learning. It may be only when communicating with other professionals that we need to commit information to paper. It takes a great deal of skill and practice to present detailed observations succinctly.

TIME SAMPLING

When using the Tavistock Method, there is usually a time boundary of an hour a week for the observation to be made. This is similar to 'time sampling' as described in the literature about observation (Fawcett, 1996, p. 59). In settings, we often try to gather information over a whole session or day. Isaacs tried to gain as full a picture as possible of how the children were engaging in her setting.

At the Pen Green Nursery each child is the 'focus' of everyone's attention about once every six weeks. The focus children's names (two each session) are displayed on the large whiteboards in the main nursery rooms and it is everyone's responsibility to write about, photograph or film what they see those children engaging in throughout a whole morning or afternoon. In addition, workers spontaneously record anything they consider notable that any child engages in.

EVENT SAMPLING

Another way of managing observations is to sample certain events that are of interest to us (Fawcett, 1996, p. 60; Podmore, 2006, p. 42). At the Pen Green Centre, we have always been most interested in what the children **choose** to do and in how they play with each other, with adults and with the resources available to them. We are less interested in observing adult-led activities which we think may offer less insight into the children's interests, thinking and motivations.

At the start of the project on children's well-being and resilience, we filmed a small number of children being settled in to nursery by their parents/carers and at reunion (an event sample). This is because we were interested in 'attachment' and in what sorts of things helped the children to feel secure at nursery (Bowlby, 1998). We went on to film children in 20–30-minute blocks (a time sample) during their nursery session, usually once a week. We found this filming very valuable as it enabled us to reflect on development and learning alongside children and their families.

INTERPRETING OBSERVATIONS USING SCHEMA THEORY AND ATTACHMENT THEORY

For this smaller study of eight children, I decided to use schema theory and attachment theory to make links and to deepen my understanding of the children's actions. It was only when we began to put together our observations of children's repeated patterns of action (schemas) with information from home, particularly in relation to separation, attachment and loss, that we began to gather evidence of a possible link between schemas explored and emotions experienced, across the group of children.

'CONTENT' AND 'FORM'

It seems important to note that when we are thinking about extending thought in young children by 'feeding' their current schemas, we are thinking about the 'form' rather than the 'content'. Traditionally, in settings, we have been concerned with offering 'content', for example, to extend an interest in clocks, we might offer a range of timepieces (related 'content'). Observation of the underlying 'form' might reveal an interest in <u>rotation</u>. Many more experiences could be offered to support and extend children's interest in <u>rotation</u> and <u>circularity</u>.

SCHEMAS OBSERVED

The following observable patterns of repeated actions were seen in the study of children's behaviour:

- Lines – making lines with objects or string.

- Trajectory – moving in or representing straight lines, arcs or curves.

- Oblique trajectory – moving in, using or drawing oblique lines.

- Dab – making a stabbing trajectory movement, sometimes resulting in a mark.

- Connecting and disconnecting – connecting themselves to objects and objects to each other and disconnecting.

- Proximity and separation – before children can connect, they sometimes place objects or marks in 'proximity' to each other or represent them separately (Athey, 2007, p. 73).

- Enclosure – enclosing oneself, an object or space.

- Enveloping – enveloping or covering oneself, an object or space.

- Containing – putting materials or oneself inside an object capable of containing them or objects.

- Inside – being interested in the inside space of a container.

- Subdivision of space – being interested in the subdivision of space, for example, upstairs and downstairs.

- Transporting – carrying objects or being carried from one place to another.

- Going through a boundary – causing oneself or some material to go through a boundary and emerge at the other side.

- Classification – when objects, people or materials are grouped according to their similarities. The classifications become increasingly refined.

- Seriation – ordering objects or people according to size or other comparative features.

- Rotation – turning, twisting or rolling oneself or objects around.

- Circularity – the shape made through rotation.

- Grid – vertical and horizontal parallel lines or bars, which intersect at right angles to each other.

- Positioning – children position themselves and objects in different ways, thereby gaining different views of the world and of objects. Some objects can be placed in vertical, horizontal or oblique positions.

- Core with radials – a co-ordination of a central core (enclosure) with radial appendages (trajectories).

- Transformation (not a repeated pattern but an aspect observed – transformation occurs as a result of some action, for example, sand becomes soggy as a result of adding water to it) – transforming oneself by dressing differently or being interested in changes of state. Definitions from Arnold (1997, pp. 45–8).

Some of these repeated patterns seemed to be more readily understood as part of children's emotional lives, for example, transporting objects from home to nursery offered John security and sometimes related to 'transitional objects' as described by Winnicott (1991, p. 4). Winnicott described transitional objects as the first 'not-me possession', 'a defence against anxiety' and acknowledged that they were symbolic of the mother. Spotting children using schemas at a symbolic representation level was significant in our study.

Piaget, himself, acknowledged that 'The schemas relative to persons are cognitive and affective simultaneously. The affective element is perhaps more important in the domain of persons and the cognitive element in the domain of things, but it is only a question of degree' (1962, p. 95).

Piaget talked about 'conscious and unconscious symbolism' and gave examples of when a child might consciously be using one object to represent another. He observed his daughter, Jacqueline, aged 1 year 10 months, 'using a shell on a box to represent a cat on a wall'. She said 'cat on the wall' demonstrating her conscious use of symbols (1951, p. 171). In contrast, Piaget pointed out examples of when a child does not understand the significance of his own actions, for example,

> A child who has been made jealous by the birth of a younger brother and happens to be playing with two dolls of unequal size, will make the smaller one go away on a journey, while the bigger one stays with his mother. Assuming that the child is unaware that he is thinking of his younger brother and himself, we shall call a case of this kind secondary or unconscious symbolism. (1951, p. 171)

Similarly, when observing my grandson, Harry, 'playing with Teddy Tom' (a small teddy): 'Harry carried Tom carefully, saying "He's got no daddy", then "he's got no mummy" – "no brothers, no sisters"' (Arnold, 2003, p. 60). Harry was 2 years 10 months and this was a few weeks after his parents had told him and his sister that they were going to separate. I deduced from this that Harry was using Teddy Tom to express his own anxiety and fear of abandonment, and that this deeper meaning was out of his conscious awareness. It was often clearer to us, as parents and workers, when children 'projected' their feelings on to toys, particularly toys that could represent people. In her study, Janet Shaw concluded that 'An infant's concept of objects is initially formed through the projection onto them of aspects of her inner life ... Symbolising anxiety through projection onto objects provided the child with a defence against directly experiencing the anxiety' (1991, p. 364).

We were also searching for instances where the link was less easily made, such as when Harry was <u>connecting</u> with string and not necessarily verbalising and animating his thoughts and feelings about his actions.

USING ATTACHMENT THEORY TO UNDERSTAND CHILDREN'S ACTIONS

Many hundreds of studies of 'attachment' have been made across cultures and have considered various aspects of attachment, separation and loss (Cassidy and Shaver, 1999). Mary Ainsworth et al. (1978) developed 'a laboratory procedure that was designed to capture the balance of attachment and exploratory behaviour under conditions of increasing though moderate stress' (Solomon and George, 1999, p. 290). They noticed that children's behaviour, at reunion with their parents or carers, after a short separation, was significant and seemed to follow certain patterns. Their finding was that children were either: 'securely attached to mother', 'anxiously attached to mother and avoidant' or 'anxiously attached to mother and resistant' (Bowlby, 1997, p. 338). Subsequently Main and Solomon added a fourth category of attachment behaviour, described as 'disorganised or disoriented' (Solomon and George, 1999, p. 291).

Although we were interested in these findings, it was not our intention to make judgements about the security of individuals' attachment to their parents or workers. There was overwhelming evidence to suggest that, as human beings, we are all affected by our early experiences, particularly in relation to separation, attachment, loss and transitions. As parents and nursery practitioners, we wanted to use the research to help us understand when children's security was threatened and how we could help. Attachment theory provided the concepts and language to be able to discuss such issues. In a way, we were trying to bring into our conscious awareness the possibility that children might be exploring issues to do with separation and attachment.

SO WHAT?

Sir Isaac Newton said in 1675 'If I have seen further it is by standing on the shoulders of giants'.

In some ways, we were feeling our way with this study. The tradition of Child Study in both early education and psychoanalysis offered us 'shoulders to stand on'. We also used our own experiences of relating to children and their families over a number of years. We knew that using video was important and, particularly in a study of emotions, would provide a way of revisiting and re-experiencing what happened.

Certain aspects are important if our observations are to be timeless:

■ Stating the exact age of each child in years, months and days enables us to recognise development over time.

■ Giving the context of an observation helps others to understand what's going on.

■ Stating the time and duration of an observation also helps to communicate how important the concern or exploration was and how persistent children have been in pursuing a concern or interest.

■ Written observations must communicate with others. That is the main purpose and communicating clearly takes a great deal of skill and practice. Photographs can help with communication.

- If video observations are made, they need to be labelled in some way with the date and time. Watching and editing video takes time and those processes need to be manageable for workers during the normal working day.

- Even 2 or 3 minutes of video can demonstrate a great deal and can be used in training or to share with parents.

At the Pen Green Nursery, we are constantly striving to improve our methods of observation and communication. We are interested in what each child brings to the learning situation, and observing the children closely can give us insights into **their agenda** and the possibilities for development and learning. One technique we are currently using is an observation sheet to make sure that all essential information is recorded. An important aspect is reflecting together with parents about what their child is trying to understand or learn about. A second technique is to use a Possible Lines of Development chart (Figures 1.1 and 1.2), which is a sort of medium-term plan, starting with the child or children's interests at the centre. I cannot emphasise too strongly that we are seeking to understand which interests and schemas children are exploring. We cannot decide in advance what they will learn but 'feeding' their current schemas seems to go some way towards helping children to learn in a deep way.

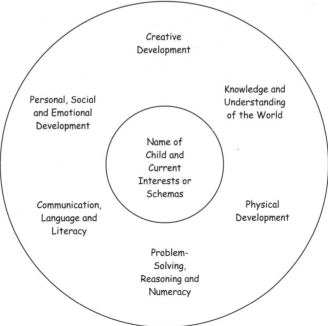

Figure 1.1 Possible Lines of Development chart
Source: Pen Green Team, 2009

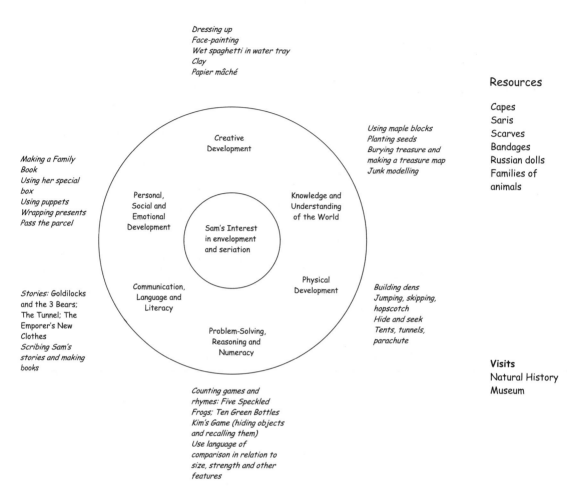

Figure 1.2 Possible Lines of Development chart for Sam
Source: Pen Green Team, 2009

SUGGESTED FURTHER READING

Fawcett, M. (1996) *Learning Through Child Observation*, Jessica Kingsley, London.

Isaacs, S. (1930/1966) *Intellectual Growth in Young Children*, Routledge and Kegan Paul, London.

Isaacs, S. (1933) *Social Development in Young Children*, George Routledge and Sons, London.

Johnson, H. (1928/1972) *Children in The Nursery School*, Agathon Press, New York.

Pen Green Nursery Observation Sheet (currently in use)

Part One: Narrative Observation – Telling the Story

Name:

Date of birth/Age:

Date, time and length of observation:

Place:

How did the child get involved?

What happened next?

Part Two: Reflective Practice

What does the play/investigation seem to be about?

How did you support the play?

What new/supporting language did you introduce?

What learning do you consider took place?

Schemas	Involvement	Well-being	Pedagogic Stategies

Links to the Curriculum Framework

Possible Extensions

2

Ewan: Developing a Ritual for Separating

In this chapter we introduce:

- Ewan and his family
- Observations of Ewan separating from his mother
- Observations of Ewan at other times

INTRODUCTION AND CONTEXT

Ewan lived locally with his mum, dad and older brother, who had also attended the nursery. Ewan's parents were very involved in his education and supportive of the nursery. Ewan attended the nursery for two years. He was later than his brother in using expressive language and this caused his parents some anxiety during his first year at nursery. However, Ewan could communicate well and had a good understanding of what was said to him. His parents were very keen to support his language development and when he did begin to express himself, he was very articulate and had a wide knowledge of vocabulary, stories and songs.

Ewan's family were involved in the Well-being and Resilience Study right at the beginning. We began by filming Ewan settling in to nursery and at his reunion with each of his parents. We then viewed the filmed material with his Family Worker (Key Worker), Annette, and his parents to interpret what was going on for him at those times.

We found that each of the children studied had their own unique way of separating from their parents at nursery each day. Ewan seemed to need to go through a sort of ritual before he was happy to let his mum or dad leave him at nursery. We were keen to know about and understand the different ways that children settled away from their parents.

Subsequently, we filmed Ewan at different times during the day, playing outside, on the computer, in the block area and at Family Grouptime. Again, we viewed the filmed material with his Family Worker and parents to gain insights.

We have drawn on these video observations to raise questions and to give possible interpretations of Ewan's actions.

Observation: Ewan separating from his mum and brother

Ewan (2:10:23) came into the nursery with his mum, and his older brother. He 'settled' at the marble run with his Family Worker, Annette. Ewan knelt on the floor facing Annette. The marble run was between them. Ewan seemed very engaged with putting marbles in the top of the run and watching them run through to the base of the run. His mother came from behind and rubbed/patted his back, kissed him and told him she needed to go to work. He did not respond ... She seemed a little unsure but walked slowly towards the door. Seconds passed before he turned around and shouted 'Mum'. He got up quickly and took Annette's hand and walked to the door, where his mother was waiting. She crouched down facing him and held him and kissed him and then said 'Bye bye'. He turned back and walked back to the space he had left looking satisfied and sure of himself.

DISCUSSION AND INTERPRETATION OF EWAN'S ACTIONS AND COMMUNICATION

When we discussed this observation, both his mother and Annette said that it was important for Ewan to carry out his 'goodbye ritual', which included going to the door and seeing his mother or father go. He also developed, over time, a bedtime ritual, which included his mother saying 'Night, night, sweet dreams – see you in the morning'. His mother had to say these words in the same order each night or he would get up or shout down to her to repeat the words correctly.

In terms of attachment theory, it seemed that seeing his parents go enabled Ewan to focus on becoming involved with peers and in other activities. He seemed secure to explore once he knew his parents had gone. Ewan's parents told me that he carried out similar actions at home. If his dad was going to work, he would say goodbye at the back door but then dash to the front window to wave and see him disappear down the road.

Although we talked about 'Ewan's need' for a ritualistic separation at the time, it is important to acknowledge that it was a ritual negotiated between two or more people. In this observation his mother was waiting. She knew how important it was for Ewan to say that final goodbye at the door to outside and to see her go. Annette, too, was prepared to rush to the door with Ewan. In good nursery practice, we emphasise 'knowing each child and family' (Carr, 2001; Whalley, 1997, 2007) and 'Do you know how I like to settle in each day?' is an important part of that knowing.

We also discussed the possible significance of Ewan's play with the marble run in terms of schemas. Ewan used the marble run, which could be symbolic of his mother disappearing or leaving and reappearing or coming back. The marbles 'go through a boundary' and run in lines and circles to the base. Ewan seemed to give some attention to what the marbles looked like when they formed a complete circle at the base of the run. While he was engaged with the run, he almost forgot (?) to carry out the sequence of actions he, himself, had developed in order to have some control over the separation. The sequence of actions somehow marked Ewan's transition from home or from being with his parents to being at nursery with other people and engaging in different activities. The marbles 'going through' the run could alternatively be a representation of Ewan himself, going from one place to another through a series of twists and turns.

The complete circle formed by the marbles at the base of the run may somehow have represented completion or wholeness. Completing a perfect circle was understandably satisfying to the eye, and understanding that his mum would leave, go to work and return may have been satisfying to Ewan in emotional terms.

The fact that his mother 'held' him at the doorway may have been significant too. Winnicott talked about the concept of feeling safely 'held' physically and also emotionally 'held', as in, held together and without a feeling of falling apart emotionally (Winnicott, 2006, p. 26). Holding Ewan one last time before leaving may have reminded him that he was held in mind by his parents and that they trusted others to hold him while they were at work.

We wondered whether Ewan's use of a separation ritual was reflected in his play with objects later on that morning.

Observation: Later that morning

Mid-session, Ewan was filmed completing a perfectly symmetrical building with maple blocks. He went on to place seven large cylindrical blocks in a line closely connected to each other on top of the building. He made no comment about his building.

DISCUSSION AND INTERPRETATION OF EWAN'S ACTIONS AND COMMUNICATION

Other observations made at that time indicated that Ewan frequently placed objects in <u>lines</u>. <u>Lines</u> enabled Ewan to explore space. In view of Ewan's separation ritual, we wondered whether he was exploring time as well as space. Ewan was at the stage of understanding that he stayed at the nursery for the morning. During that space of time, there were some markers. He engaged in different activities with different people. He helped himself to snacks and a drink when he chose to. Annette gathered his group for stories and songs, and then his mother or father would come to pick him up and take him home.

In a similar way, Ewan had negotiated a ritual to mark the departure of his parents. So maybe this sequencing in <u>lines</u> was helping him to understand the sequence of past and future events.

Time is a difficult concept for young children to understand and, as Shaw has pointed out, closely linked to separation from important people (Shaw, 1991, 2005). As adults, we represent time spatially so it may be reasonable to suppose that an interest in closely connected lines helps children with the abstract concept of time as well as helping to work through and understand the concept of separation.

In attachment terms, the close connection of the blocks might represent the continuity or smoothness of the transition. Ewan may have been working through or using the '<u>line</u>' at a symbolic level to understand the continuity of his separation and <u>connectedness</u> to people at nursery.

Winnicott (1975, p. 124) talked about a child he had been treating, who returned to the clinic and constructed 'a very long road with toy houses'. His interpretation, in this instance, was that she 'was joining up the past with the present, joining my house with her own, integrating past experience with present'. So maybe Ewan's <u>line</u> was <u>connecting</u> past and present, present and future, home and nursery.

Ewan also seemed to be interested in <u>lines</u> of words that connected with each other.

An observation at grouptime

Ewan (3:0:17) was filmed participating in action rhymes during grouptime. He seemed happy and engaged when standing on top of a chair. He particularly enjoyed the phrase 'knocked at the door with a rat tat tat'. He became concerned when playing 'Sleeping Bunnies' and two of the children stayed lying down and did not follow the sequence of actions. When this happened a second time, he removed himself from the game and sat on a computer chair nearby.

DISCUSSION AND INTERPRETATION OF EWAN'S ACTIONS AND COMMUNICATION

In this observation at grouptime, Ewan enjoyed participating in the action rhymes but moved away when two children did not complete the sequence of actions. There was a kind of 'form' to the sequence of actions, like the 'line' of cylinders or the sequence of actions that made up Ewan's ritualistic separation. He seemed to be showing some dissatisfaction with the children stopping part of the way through.

We began to think about the purpose of Ewan's ritual. The ritual gave 'form' or introduced order into an event that may have been highly emotionally charged. It meant that Ewan could predict and trust what would happen. In a similar way, action rhymes are repeated and predictable. The predictability of events can help us to feel safe and secure. When we are first learning any new skill, it is harder to deviate from a plan. As we become more experienced and confident in knowing a plan, we can 'play' with our ideas and make changes and adapt to the unexpected (Athey, 2007, p. 51).

Once Ewan felt secure about what would happen, he could adapt his actions to 'accommodate' to different circumstances.

Observation: Ewan separating from his mum at the gym

There was extensive building work in the nursery and the nursery population (children and adults) had to move into the gym for three months. Ewan found this frustrating, first in terms of understanding what was happening, and secondly in terms of carrying out the ritual he and his parents had established.

By then Ewan (3:6:0) was talking but not understanding how 'nursery', as he knew it, could be in the gym. Everything was different, the acoustics, the entrance after walking along a corridor, the garden. Ewan got quite cross when adults referred to the gym as though it was nursery. It was impossible for children to move freely indoors and out. Adults had to accompany the children into the garden. Instead of children sometimes settling out of doors first thing in the morning, the adults and children had to adapt and say their goodbyes in the gym, before being accompanied to the garden in small groups.

As far as his goodbye ritual was concerned, Ewan had to adapt it. He could say his goodbye at the door to the gym, but then he would dash over to the opposite wall, stack a pile of heavy hollow blocks against the wall and climb up so that he could see his mum or dad through the high window, disappearing. He would give them a final wave.

DISCUSSION AND INTERPRETATION OF EWAN'S ACTIONS AND COMMUNICATION

In terms of schemas, Ewan seemed to know that being able to wave his parents off at the very high window of the gym was 'functionally dependent' on placing a tower of blocks underneath the window and climbing on top of them (Athey, 1990, p. 70). He used his experience of <u>lines</u> to create a <u>vertical line</u> high enough to reach the window. At this stage, everything had changed and although Ewan was disequilibrated by not being able to carry out his usual goodbye, he was able to 'accommodate' his actions and ideas to a whole new situation (Piaget, 1950/2001, p. 8).

In attachment terms, he still seemed to need to see them disappear in order to trust that they had gone and would return later. So he retained that part of the ritual and fulfilling that goal seemed to satisfy him.

When the children and workers returned to the nursery, Ewan made another adaptation to his sequence of actions around separation.

Observation: Ewan separating from his mum outside

Ewan (3:8:29) asked Annette to go outside to the perimeter fence with him. He kissed his mother through the railings at one end, then raced to the middle for another kiss through the railings and, finally, ran again to the end of the railings for a final kiss and goodbye. He then walked back towards nursery holding Annette's hand.

DISCUSSION AND INTERPRETATION OF EWAN'S ACTIONS AND COMMUNICATION

Ewan enjoyed playing outside and, as outdoor play was usually available to the children right through the session, this extension of his ritual/goodbye routine may have developed out of his wish to say a 'goodbye' at the final boundary (?). Again, he seemed to have a sense of satisfaction when he had completed the ritual.

In schema terms, Ewan may just have discovered that he could kiss his mum or dad by <u>going through</u> the fence with his face/lips. Like all new learning, he may have wanted to practise using his <u>going through a boundary</u> schema.

In attachment terms, the boundary seemed important to Ewan. Was he creating ever more final points at which the goodbye could be said? His mum worked at the school opposite the nursery and that meant that her workplace could be seen from the nursery garden. Did sight of the school provide even more security?

Boundaries seemed to link with his interest at grouptime later that day.

Observation at grouptime later that day

Ewan was filmed at grouptime and enjoyed singing 'Wind the Bobbin Up' which his mother told me was a favourite song of his at the time. It is interesting to think about the words:

Point to the ceiling

Point to the door

Point to the window

Point to the floor ...

DISCUSSION AND INTERPRETATION OF EWAN'S ACTIONS AND COMMUNICATION

In terms of Ewan's wish to say goodbye at the furthest boundary, these words might have been significant or resonated with him. Athey noticed that articulating children's schemas/repeated actions seemed to help them form related concepts (Athey, 1990, p. 179). Athey (1990, p. 181) noted that 'children like to talk about what they are doing'.

John Matthews, drawing on brain research, gives a further explanation about the importance of language in forming concepts:

> There are two types of basic attractor systems (in the brain) set off with emergent representation. One traces around the contours of shapes in terms of action, while another system records the features of objects. Gradually, the child learns the names for shapes ('round' for example) and this word may cause families of attractors to form around it. The **word acts like a 'pivot'** around which utterances, and linguistic, visual and kinaesthetic representations (to do with movement and the sensation of movement), are formed. (2003, p. 29, author's emphasis)

I understand this to mean that language acts as a symbol and helps us to recall all related experiences of our actions. Language helps us to conceptualise and to communicate about concepts with each other. Ewan's many experiences of forming <u>lines</u> could be recalled by the word 'line'.

A final observation at grouptime

By now Ewan (4:3:21) was like a 'fish in water' at nursery, extremely articulate and enjoyed playing with words. He really enjoyed 'The Owl and the Pussycat' and Annette read part of each line which Ewan completed. He particularly liked saying 'quince'. He also joked with his friend, Owen, saying 'willy' instead of 'willing'.

DISCUSSION AND INTERPRETATION OF EWAN'S ACTIONS AND COMMUNICATION

By then, Ewan was feeling very confident and secure at nursery. He loved to experiment with new words, stories and rhymes. He also liked to push boundaries and to make up jokes. Like some of the children in Athey's study, his jokes demonstrated that he knew things so well that he could play with them.

SO WHAT?

Getting to know Ewan was important to him and to his family. They all felt more valued in a place where people listened and took note of what was important to Ewan and to them. Ewan had negotiated and developed a way of separating from his parents that made the separation manageable for him and them at that time. The ritual was created by Ewan in negotiation with others. He must have felt valued as a person, in his own right, when those around him thought of the ritual as useful and acknowledged its importance to him. I am sure that at times, carrying out a ritual, created stress for the family, however, the filmed sequence of Ewan walking back into nursery after being 'held' by his mum, indicated a high level of emotional well-being and self confidence (Laevers, 1997).

We can apply our learning from this child study to other children and families. I believe that if we notice and understand what is of importance to each child and family using our setting, then their experience can only improve.

We, too, can introduce rituals to help children cope with separations or endings, for example, when it was approaching the ending of a group for very young children and their parents called 'Growing Together' we marked the approach of the ending by blowing bubbles. Even the youngest children attending became used to the idea that after the bubbles, they went home.

Table 2.1 Schemas mentioned and links made

Going through a boundary	Ewan repeatedly used marbles in a run to go through a series of twists and turns
Lines	Ewan seemed to use lines and may have been representing time, closely linked with separation, connecting past and present, home and nursery
Connecting	Ewan was interested in connecting, which may have linked with connecting with others and smoothness of transitions
Vertical lines	Ewan constructed a vertical line/tower in order to reach a high window and making it possible to wave 'Goodbye' at the last possible moment

SUGGESTED FURTHER READING

Athey, C. (1990) *Extending Thought in Young Children*, Paul Chapman, London.

Athey, C. (2007) *Extending Thought in Young Children*, 2nd edn, Paul Chapman, London.

Matthews, J. (2003) *Drawing and Painting: Children and Visual Representation*, Paul Chapman, London.

Winnicott, D. (2006) *The Family and Individual Development*, Routledge Classics, London.

3

John: Exploring Lines and Connecting and Coming to Understand Separations

This chapter introduces:

- John and his family
- Observations of John 'connecting' with adults, using string
- Observations of John's reactions to his mum and sister leaving nursery without him

INTRODUCTION AND CONTEXT

John and his family lived locally. He attended the nursery for two years and was the third child in his family to come to the nursery and use other services in the centre.

John is one of five children within a reconstituted family. He has an older half-brother and an older half-sister who both live with their biological father but spend time once or twice a week in John's family home with their mother. John also has an older half-sister who lives with her biological mother and spends time each week in John's family home with her father. John also has a younger sister. John has a very close relationship with his father.

We were concerned when we first observed John, that he was fairly unfocused for some of the time, in the nursery environment. He lay down drinking from a bottle and twiddling his hair, not making eye contact with me or with others. Within three months of those initial observations, John was assigned a one-to-one support worker to support him in becoming more involved with other people at nursery.

During the course of this study, John was formally diagnosed as being on the autistic spectrum. We were a little concerned about his responses to other people, as a young infant and by the time of this study, his parents and workers were showing grave concern about John's lack of interactions and communication. Rodier (2000, p. 42) defines autism, 'A diagnosis of autism requires that the patient exhibit abnormal behaviours in 3 categories: Impairment of Social Interaction; Impairment of Communication; Restricted and Repetitive Interests and Behaviours'.

As we were not specialists in this area, we want to emphasise that we were approaching the study of John as we would any other child. We were interested in what was unique to him but also searching for generalisable findings, that might be applicable to other children. However, we also needed to take into account the research of specialists in autistic behaviour. Rodier (2000, p. 45) states that tests on children with autism 'show a tendency to focus on one stimulus and a failure to disengage from that first stimulus'. This was particularly contentious in terms of observing 'schemas' or repeated patterns of action in John's explorations. Not only were these repeated actions sometimes considered by special educational needs workers to be an abnormal feature, but they were often discouraged by workers, concerned with helping children to move on or progress. However, there was some guidance from specialists that 'Obsessions should not be "stamped out" but extended creatively, where possible, and others replaced with behaviour that serves the same purpose for the child' (Jordan and Powell, 1995, p. 49).

So we were prepared to be open to observing John's actions and to using information from his parents and workers to understand those actions. We also had an ongoing dialogue with Dr Jean-Marc Michel, our local paediatrician, who has a particular interest in autism (Michel and Arnold, 2005). During our discussions, we agreed that identifying schemas seemed to give us some insights into John's intentions. This helped us to understand some of what he was trying to learn about. The most difficult aspect was that John was using very little expressive language and often seemed not to respond to other people. We had to become much better at identifying subtle changes in his behaviour or body language to understand what John was feeling or expressing.

I sat next to John at lunch for two years and, therefore, gathered a great deal of extra information about his interests and progress.

When John was first observed, he used to bring his bottle containing milk to nursery from home and use it as an 'object of transition' (Bruce, 2001, p. 77). He would carry it about, sometimes using it in his play and sometimes drinking from it. With regard to Winnicott's work on 'transitional phenomena', we have always acknowledged the emotional significance of objects brought from home to nursery and taken from nursery to home (Pen Green Team, 2004). These objects do not necessarily serve the same function as the 'transitional object' that according to Winnicott (1975, p. 236) 'stands for the breast, or the object of the first relationship'. We knew that John used his bottle as an 'object of transition', connecting home and nursery. The bottle may also have been a 'transitional object', John's first 'Not-me' possession as described by Winnicott, that was enabling him to exert his power over an object (1975, p. 230).

John's parents were advised by medical specialists to wean him from his bottle as he was using it to 'dumb' his frustration when he could not communicate his needs. His parents had the idea of placing beads in his bottle instead of milk. This change meant that John could continue to '<u>transport</u>' his bottle to nursery with him and he continued to do this for a few weeks.

At home, John began playing with an old computer lead. The lead gradually seemed to replace John's need to carry his bottle and he began taking it to bed with him and '<u>transporting</u>' the lead to nursery each day. He would play with the lead, sometimes using it like a washing line and <u>connecting</u> pegs to it. John seemed to be combining '<u>transporting</u>', '<u>connecting</u>' and <u>lines</u>. John also began playing with string at nursery.

At this time, John rarely initiated interactions with other children or adults. So it was quite a surprise to us and to John's parents when he was filmed interacting with a researcher and using string to <u>connect</u> with her.

Observation: Using string with Colette

At 3:00:14 (3 years and 14 days) John was filmed taking a small ball of string out of a drawer, unravelling it and offering one end to a researcher, Colette.

(Continued)

(Continued)

Colette stayed where she was standing up and holding the string, while John backed away from her and held the string above his head and taut.

He dropped the string several times but, each time, came forward and, giggling, retrieved it and again held it high above his head. He looked up at the line he and Colette were creating. When Colette dropped her end, he giggled and jumped up and down. He picked up the other end and gave it to Colette again.

At one point, John dropped his end and another child, Ben, picked it up. John looked at him, clasped his hands together, turned and walked away. Then turned back towards Ben and squealed with what may have been frustration (?)

Colette intervened, asking Ben to let John have his string back. John resumed his game of extending the string, holding it high above his head and looking up at the line he was creating.

Then suddenly John ran towards Ben and threw both arms around him. Ben looked distressed and said 'You are all wet John'. Colette said twice 'John, I don't think Ben wants you to do that'. John moved away and again resumed holding the line of string above his head.

DISCUSSION AND INTERPRETATION OF JOHN'S ACTIONS AND COMMUNICATION

In schema theory terms, John's concerns could be described as '<u>proximity</u>' and '<u>separation</u>', '<u>connecting</u>' and '<u>lines</u>', important for mathematical understanding of length, distance, connecting points in space and mapping.

In attachment theory terms, <u>connecting</u> and <u>disconnecting</u> with string could represent John's attachment to and separation from other people. Taking account of John's sociocultural context: he lived in a household where there was a lot of, sometimes unpredictable, coming and going each week. His older half-siblings were there sometimes but not always. He sometimes played with his older sister, but always wanted to be with his dad.

John was unsure about how to interact with the other children at nursery. He demonstrated his uncertainty when Ben picked up the string he was using. John seemed not to know what to do. His initial reaction was to turn away. He was attempting interactions that were not successful and he could not verbalise his needs.

There was a delay between Ben giving John his string back, at Colette's request, and John 'throwing his arms around Ben' although one action may have led to the other. Soale (2004) reported a delay in her son's reactions to others, showing that this was an aspect of autism as shown in her child's behaviour. Was John out of synergy with the world?

It may not have been a coincidence that he chose to '<u>connect</u>' with another person through using string, which may have been less of a risk for him. Perhaps John could only express his wish to be connected to other people through using available objects, such as string.

He chose Colette, an adult and a researcher, who knew his family well and had known him from birth. In terms of what he was trying to do with the string, an adult, whom he knew well and trusted, was more likely to follow his lead than another child. Keeping the string taut in a <u>line</u> between them seemed most important to John.

He subsequently used this technique with another adult.

Observation: Using the computer lead to connect with Cath

I filmed John (3:4:29) at lunchtime. He carried his computer lead from home, with about thirty pegs attached, into lunch and kept it on the table near him. After lunch and some songs, John placed one end of the lead into my hand and walked towards the door. I allowed him to 'lead' and, as always, he stopped just before the threshold for a few seconds, before stepping through the doorway to the covered area and outside … he led me to a small trike and wound his end of the lead around the handlebar and scooted along leading me behind him.

He stopped at one point. He noticed one of the pegs, on its own, away from the other pegs on his line, and moved it along next to the others.

John continued scooting around the playground, leading me. I said 'John, can I let go of this now? Can I put it on the ground and let it trail?' (as I placed my end of the lead on the ground). I explained "Cos I need to go in a minute. I need to go back to my work in a minute'. He stopped and then rode forward a few

(Continued)

(Continued)

yards before stopping and turning around and looking at the lead on the ground. He got off the trike, picked up the end of the lead and placed it into my hand, saying 'Te Ta'. I said 'You want me to hold it?' as he got on the trike and scooted away.

He rode away quite quickly and I dropped my end saying 'I dropped it! Sorry John I dropped it – shall I pick it up?' He stopped and looked down at the lead. I picked it up and he carried on, more slowly this time.

John stopped and I asked 'Do you want me to ask someone else to hold this as I have to go back to my work now. Who would you like to hold it?' As John reached the bottom of the ramp, his end of the lead unravelled from the handle of the trike and fell to the ground. I picked it up and gave it to him. He began winding it around the middle of the handle bar, singing 'Ma ma mu' to the tune of 'Frère Jacques' as he did it.

He rode away again leading me. I asked 'Shall I ask Michelle (adult) to hold it?' One of the other children, Courtney, offered, so I gave my end to her. John said 'Bye bye' and made an awkward looking side to side movement with his hand. He walked alongside his trike leading Courtney by wheeling the trike but not getting onto it.

DISCUSSION AND INTERPRETATION OF JOHN'S ACTIONS AND COMMUNICATION

In this observation John demonstrated his strong urge to '<u>connect</u>' his lead to the trike by '<u>rotating</u>' the lead several times around the handle bars to '<u>enclose</u>' and secure it. Keeping the lead securely connected to the handle bars was 'functionally dependent' on wrapping it around several times (Athey, 1990, p. 69). These sorts of actions are precursors to tying knots and frequently observed in children of this age (Arnold, 2003, p. 117).

John's other concern was that I should be 'connected' to him through holding the lead. Bowlby (1997, p. 181) described attachment as 'proximity-seeking behaviour' and the function was protection from predators. There was no way that John needed physical protection on this occasion but he did, for 10 minutes or more, engage in behaviour designed to prolong my presence and avoid separating from me. In a chapter on 'Attachment in children with autism' Yirmiya and Sigman (2001, p. 57) state that although 'Children with autism looked less frequently at their mother, smiled less and showed her objects less often … there were no significant differences in approaching the mother' and, therefore, these children are just as likely to be securely attached as the general population. They argued that 'their attachment is in the service of the self; it is self-enhancing and does not necessarily take into account the other as a separate self with a separate mind that needs to be related to' (2001, p. 61).

A small but possibly significant act, was pushing a peg nearer to the rest of the pegs, showing that he wanted to place it in close proximity to the other pegs. This small act could have signified an interest in sets, parts of a whole or his own proximity to other people.

When his end of the lead unravelled, John became very 'involved' in securing it again (Laevers, 1997). He hummed the tune to 'Frère Jacques', a tune his father frequently sang to him. He seemed content and at peace with himself as he engaged in securing the lead to his trike. Maybe this was something he had done several times before and knew he could achieve and, therefore, was satisfying.

When I dropped the lead, John seemed to understand that me keeping hold of the lead was 'functionally dependent' on him riding more slowly. I was filming as well as interacting with John which made it more difficult for me to move quickly.

When I finally handed over my end of the lead to Courtney, John showed he understood I was leaving by saying 'Bye bye' and waving. Unlike most young children, John rarely waved or acknowledged that people were leaving. He was more inclined to seem to ignore or not notice them leaving.

Another small difference I noticed was that John led the trike by holding the handle bars and walking alongside, when Courtney had the other end of the lead. Was he distancing himself further from her or less able to trust her to stay connected?

Bowlby (1997, p. 82) said that children build up 'internal working models' based on their early interactions with other people. Did John have some kind of a model of other children arriving and leaving rather unpredictably and, therefore, not to be relied on? Yirmiya and Sigman (2001, p. 60) suggested that 'children with autism show the most difficulty with behaviours that necessitate a working model of the self and the other and their interdependence'.

When thinking about this observation, at first I experienced some tension between following John's lead and my own constraints, for example, separating from him when I needed to. He could not just say 'Please stay' and I could not tell him 'OK I'll stay for 5 minutes more and I'll see you tomorrow' as I would with any other child. I felt rather guilty that I could not stay indefinitely. I felt frustrated in not knowing how much he understood of what I said. However, on further reflection, I realised that John did understand I was going and, unusually, he acknowledged my imminent departure on this occasion by waving and saying 'Bye bye'. I also began to think that it might be helpful to John to practise the ritual involved in separating from other people. He seemed not to notice when his mum or dad left. Perhaps I needed to talk to them about the importance of that ritual for John? Maybe we had to help John to express his feelings about separating?

John continued to be interested in <u>lines</u> and <u>connecting</u> throughout his two years at nursery. His explorations became more complex and he became frustrated when he could not secure a line that was taut. His understanding of <u>connection</u> and separation may have been further challenged when his younger sister began attending nursery.

John rarely acknowledged the arrivals or departures of important people at nursery, but we did notice a subtle change in his behaviour when his younger sister started attending nursery. Mia started attending for two mornings with lunch when John was 3:06:09. This was just a few weeks after John increased his attendance from four mornings with lunch to four full days. So, for the first time, his younger sister was spending time in the nursery while he was there and also being collected and leaving with one of his parents earlier than he was.

Observation: Mia starts attending nursery

(Research Diary)

Today was Mia's first day at nursery. John had been out on the minibus all morning. When he and the other children returned, we were already at lunch. His mum and Mia were at the next table. John did not acknowledge them at all, though he did seem to 'sneak' little glances at them (I thought so and so did Angela, who was sitting opposite John).

Soon after his mum and Mia left the lunch room, John wanted to go out. I followed (as I often do). Angela explained that the usual arrangement for Mia will be for Margaret to take her from lunch to reception and that their mother will pick her up from there, so as not to disrupt John's day.

When we went out their mother and Mia had gone. John closed the beach door and went towards the Discovery Area. He stood at the Discovery Area door. I explained we could not go out there (asbestos removal this week). Then John went

---

> to the door to reception. I said 'Are you looking for Mummy? Mummy and Mia have gone home – they'll be back for you later'. Then John went to the gate of the tower. Finally, he allowed me to take his hand and we went out to the Beach. He behaved differently there, walking all around the decking, lowering his head and standing still, looking through the glass. (I think he was searching/looking for mum?)

DISCUSSION AND INTERPRETATION OF JOHN'S ACTIONS AND COMMUNICATION

Although John did not openly acknowledge his mum's or Mia's presence at lunch, he was clearly disturbed by their presence and even more disturbed by their absence when we left the lunch room. His behaviour, though fairly subtle, showed clear signs of 'searching for mother' as described by Bowlby (1998, p. 61).

The only repeated pattern was to approach each doorway, the means to 'go through' to another area and continue or extend his search. He was clearly puzzled and also behaved quite out of character.

I felt I needed to find out why the decision had been made for Mia to be reunited with her mother away from John. I could understand that both children's needs should be considered but I thought it misguided not to allow John the experience of saying 'Goodbye' and building trust that he would be collected later on in the afternoon. He was still experiencing the loss of his mother and sister, but without explanation or ritual.

Maybe I was influenced by my own experience with my son, who found it very difficult to separate from me to go to playgroup over 30 years ago. I had found it easier to ask a friend to take Paul, so that he (and I) did not suffer the raw pain of separation. I now know that I was communicating to my son that separating was unbearable.

I needed to be careful not to muddle my pain with John's but I felt that I needed to be grounded in the learning I had gained from my own losses and to talk to workers about what was happening with John. So the next day I spoke to the workers about John's experience.

I said that I felt we should be helping him to say goodbye rather than whisking Mia and her mother away. They explained that the arrangement had been made with Mia's best interests in mind. They could, however, see that John needed support with changes and separation.

Observation: Seeing his mum and Mia leave

(Research Diary)

Two days later, Mia and her mother were in lunch again. Again John sneaked looks at them … He ran around the room and to the door several times. I said 'I'll go out with John, I've had enough sitting now'. When I opened the door, John ran back in. I went back to the table with him and said clearly 'You need to sit down at the table or go outside'. He chose to go outside.

We went to the Beach. He spent the first couple of minutes trying to run in. I closed the doors and took his hand … We watched for his mum and Mia. When they came I emphasised that they would be going home and said goodbye. His mother said 'Bye' and John saw them go through the door. I said they would be back later for John. He came back through to the Beach. (This may also link with his routine from last year when he always went home after lunch, so part of his confusion was that he was staying for a longer time.)

DISCUSSION AND INTERPRETATION OF JOHN'S ACTIONS AND COMMUNICATION

Again, John was unfocused and quite disturbed, possibly by his mum and sister being at lunch. He would not sit down but when we went outside, he tried to go back indoors. There seemed to be a sort of ambivalence or uncertainty about what would happen. He did not focus on any identifiable repeated action although I tried to engage him in play in the Beach Area.

Maybe it was unreasonable to expect him to settle to anything before he had seen his mum and sister leave. I was thinking about Ewan from Chapter 2, who always needed to see his mum or dad 'go through' the final boundary so that he knew they had left before he could settle to become involved in an activity of his choice. There was a kind of certainty about knowing someone had gone and would return at a particular time. Maybe John needed to know his mum and sister had gone?

I can remember being quite stressed by John's behaviour on days like this but I did feel strongly that I needed to help John to experience the pain of separation and survive. I was trying to be a 'container' for his pain and someone who could reassure him that he would survive the pain until his mum came back later in the day (Bion, 1962).

A few days later John was observed playing alone.

Observation: John plays 'Hello' and 'Goodbye'

Five days later, John (3:06:17) was really difficult at lunchtime. He was not interested or did not like the dinner. He got off his chair, went behind the blind, opened the door to outside and ran outside. None of the adults could engage him.

He squealed when I tried to hold him on my knee. He ran to the door and into the kitchen. He sat for dessert.

I took him outside as soon as he began getting restless after dessert. Outside he got a buggy with a baby in, and kept stopping to sit the baby up. He walked all around in the Discovery Area, looking very serious and pushing the buggy.

Then he went to the gate. He seemed frustrated that he could not open it. I tried to show him 'Turn it' but he would not look. He went through the gate and shut it and pushed the buggy around outside. Then he came back and opened the gate (he could do it from the outside by rattling the handle). He came through with the buggy and walked around the inside area again.

I heard John singing 'Hello, how are you' very softly. I joined in. Then he approached the gate again, rattled the handle but it would not open. Again, I turned the handle and said 'You need to turn it John'. He pushed his buggy through and said 'Bye bye'. He repeated the whole process again. (Playing 'Hello' and 'Goodbye'?)

DISCUSSION AND INTERPRETATION OF JOHN'S ACTIONS AND COMMUNICATION

Again, John was fairly agitated throughout lunch and found it difficult to settle. It seemed as though he needed an opportunity to play out what he was feeling and thinking about. Maybe the 'Hello' and 'Goodbye' game was his way of beginning to understand the new arrangements with Mia attending nursery some days. In attachment theory terms, he may have been rehearsing his separation from and reunion with his main attachment figures. He may even have been pretending to be his mum or dad, pushing the younger child in a buggy.

In schema theory terms, John was interested in 'going through a boundary' from one area to another (Athey, 1990, p. 156). We know from our studies of other young children that the 'subdivision' of space is often of interest to children of this age. Understanding how space is divided can lead to having an internalised map of where places are in relation to each other and also to seeing the world from other perspectives.

I constantly ask myself whether I am assuming too much in my interpretations of John's behaviour. The difficulty was in the subtlety of some of his most significant behaviours. His little voice could so easily have not been heard within the busy nursery environment. His version of 'Hello, how are you?' was sung very quietly and consisted of a 'La la' tongue movement. He said 'Bye bye' softly and never seemed to repeat it as other children would.

However, a few days later John was observed engaging in a similar game.

Observation: John pushing a trolley

A few days later, John (3:06:23) was filmed in the morning, half an hour after arriving. He was walking back through the gate pushing a play shopping trolley from outside to the Discovery Area. He shut the gate behind him. He left the trolley and went to the other gate and closed that too … John went back towards the trolley and pushed it around the seat …

John went back to the gate pushing the trolley. He touched the handle. Margaret (from the other side) said 'Do you want the door open?' Margaret said 'Door opening … door opening' as she opened it. John went through, left the trolley a couple of metres away and stood with his back against the wall and both hands behind his back.

Then he came and pushed the trolley saying 'Bye bye' quite clearly. He shut the gate and went and leant against the wall holding the handle of the trolley. He made an 'Aha' sound. Then he pushed the trolley up the kerb and closed the other gate, then went back down the kerb and back into the Discovery Area, closing both gates.

DISCUSSION AND INTERPRETATION OF JOHN'S ACTIONS AND COMMUNICATION

In schema terms, John was co-ordinating a cluster of schemas:

- <u>Transporting</u> the trolley and an apron inside it.

- <u>Trajectory</u> – walking in lines and giving attention to the up and down of the kerb, as well as opening and shutting the gates.

- <u>Going through the boundary</u> of the gateway from one area to another and back.

- <u>Contained/inside</u> – being in one area as distinct from another area.

- <u>Enclosure</u> – walking around in a full circle and getting back to where he began.

He was using a sequence of actions, including pauses, suggesting that he was possibly re-presenting symbolically, an experience he had had (Piaget, 1951, p. 162). He walked quite purposefully and with confidence, especially near the beginning, when he closed one gate and went to close the second gate.

The only other clue about what he was thinking was that definite 'Bye bye', clearly linking this play episode to the one a few days before when John used 'Hello' and 'Bye bye' in the play. Most young children would have engaged at least the adults around in playing a game like this. It seemed that John was doing this purely for himself, to work through or understand some of the interactions he had observed or experienced. So it would seem to connect with his ongoing understanding of his parents leaving him at nursery, when they picked Mia up. (Later on in the film, Mia was playing with another child in the Discovery Area, but John showed no obvious sign of recognising her.)

This was quite a brief episode but did show that John could engage in some sort of symbolic play, maybe when he needed to aid his own understanding of a situation. The big question was whether he was 'playing' being himself or being one of his parents. Being himself re-enacting a situation and rehearsing was one thing, but he could advance his thinking greatly if he was playing at being someone else.

John went on to become interested in <u>enveloping</u> himself and playing with 'here' and 'gone' in different ways. The following observation was made after lunch one day.

Observation: Playing with his dad at lunchtime

John (3:11:06) was quite difficult during lunch. When we went back into the nursery, Andy (his dad) was waiting for Mia. John reacted by saying 'Daaa' but then went past Andy and started using Maureen's Hoover. I asked Andy if he wanted to come outside. Andy encouraged John to leave the Hoover and come outside.

Outside John rode away on a bike and watched Andy from a distance. Then John came close, got off the bike and became interested in a large cardboard box which had been bashed in. Andy indicated another box which was a bit stronger. John got inside and covered himself completely. They developed a game where John climbed inside, Andy knocked on top saying 'Where's John?' and then John burst out saying 'Hello'.

After a little while Andy had to go and get Mia. I encouraged Andy to tell John he was going and to say 'Bye'. We continued with the game until I had to go. Andy told me that John is currently interested in 'going through'. He says he looks through the sleeve of his coat.

DISCUSSION AND INTERPRETATION OF JOHN'S ACTIONS AND COMMUNICATION

In schema terms, John was repeating the pattern of being completely 'enveloped' or 'contained' by the cardboard box, and then revealing himself by bursting through the lid. This interest fitted with the information Andy offered that he was interested in 'going through' and looking through his sleeve. He was enjoying using Maureen's Hoover because he could see bits of paper 'going through' the tube. These actions also link with his knot tying, when he made an enclosure and put the string or rope through to form a knot.

In terms of attachment theory, this was interesting. John obviously recognised his dad, but did not immediately approach him. In fact, he kept a distance until his dad invited him to play. I think this was different to what happened at home, when John usually wanted to play with Andy as soon as he came in.

This time the game that developed was definitely about being 'here and gone'. As this was several months later, perhaps John was now much happier to play with the idea of being here and gone.

It was good for me to see the way Andy played with John. I was puzzled that John did not approach his dad more readily but I think that's where his inflexibility came in. John was not used to seeing Andy at nursery. He was usually at work till 2 p.m. John's uncertainty seemed to be around what to do and say during interactions, and beginning an interaction is the most difficult part because of timing and monitoring or anticipating what the other person will do.

SO WHAT?

I believe that these observations of John show that he was using repeated patterns of action (schemas) to:

■ discover 'order in apparent disorder' (Bruce, 1991, p. 136)

■ initiate interactions with other people, and

■ give form to events he was struggling to understand.

Although our learning about and from John and his family cannot be generalised to other children with similar needs, we learned to notice his very subtle signs, especially with regard to his emotional discomfort and pleasure. This can help us to tune in to other children in the future. It was reassuring to notice his progress over time in relation to his conceptual understanding of separation even though he could not verbalise that understanding. We would feel more confident in the future to support the schematic explorations of children with additional needs.

Table 3.1 Schemas mentioned and links made

Transporting	John carried an 'object of transition' from home to nursery
Trajectory	John made journeys from home to nursery and back on foot. He also made journeys from one distinct area of the nursery to another
Connecting and disconnecting	John made connections with people through giving them one end of string to hold while he held the other end
Lines	John was concerned with making lines go from one point to another and from one person to another
Proximity and separation	John moved pegs close to each other on his line of string
Enclosing	John enclosed the handle of a bike with string in order to secure one end of string
Rotating	John rotated string around the handle of a bike in order to enclose and secure an end of string
Containing	John seemed interested in being inside one area as distinct from another area. John always stopped and looked down at the dividing line
Going through a boundary	John moved from one defined space through to another
Subdivision of space	John seemed interested in moving from one area to another
Enveloping	John covered himself completely to disappear and reappear linked to 'permanence of person'

SUGGESTED FURTHER READING

Athey, C. (1990) *Extending Thought in Young Children*, Paul Chapman, London.

Athey, C. (2007) *Extending Thought in Young Children*, 2nd edn, Paul Chapman, London.

Bowlby, J. (1997) *Attachment and Loss Volume 1*, Pimlico, London.

Bowlby, J. (1998) *Attachment and Loss Volume 2*, Pimlico, London.

Hobson, P. (2002) *The Cradle of Thought*, Macmillan, London.

4

Caitlin: Containing, Enveloping and Transporting

This chapter introduces:

- Caitlin and her family
- Observations of Caitlin exploring a cluster of schemas when her well-being was high
- Observations showing how Caitlin used the same cluster of schemas when her security was under threat

INTRODUCTION AND CONTEXT

Caitlin was 2 years 5 months and 20 days when I first observed her for this study. She was in her first year at nursery and was attending four afternoons a week. During her second year at nursery, she attended four full days a week.

Caitlin has an older brother Robert, who has additional needs. He displays some fairly difficult behaviours, such as putting himself in danger by going onto the road when cars are coming. At the beginning of the study period, they lived with their mother and Robert's biological father, who was Caitlin's stepfather.

Although she was one of the younger children in the nursery, Caitlin was, at this time, bright and sparky and already fiercely independent. She was able to be autonomous in exploring the workshop environment. She was also open to making relationships with other children and adults.

I noticed right from the start that Caitlin had developed strategies for getting whatever she wanted. She asked directly, usually by saying 'I want ...' but if this did not work or if she was not heard, she was capable of taking what she wanted from another child. This was not usually done with any aggression. Caitlin also defended her right to hang on to whatever she had, usually by positioning it away from other children.

Caitlin watched carefully what other children were doing and would freeze slightly if there was any sudden loud noise near her. Certain items seemed to carry power or status within the nursery population and Caitlin was particularly skilled at acquiring and using those items, for example, the phone, the most sought after high heels and the hose.

For a great deal of her time, Caitlin co-operated with a friend, either Lee or Morgan. She usually shared whatever she was playing with willingly with either friend. There was a period of time when she and Lee liked to dress up in the only two ballet tutus among the dressing up clothes. Caitlin would come into the nursery early, find the tutus and keep them ready for when Lee arrived.

Although Caitlin seemed interested in 'having' those status symbols, it was never just about having them, she was also interested in using them in her play and explorations.

At the start of the study, Caitlin used a dummy at bedtimes, although I never observed her using her dummy at nursery. Just before her third birthday, she lost her dummy and her mother told her she was getting too big for a dummy. She managed without it, but stayed up later and seemed more fearful of going to bed for a while (discussion with Caitlin's mother).

Two themes emerged from the data on Caitlin:

- An enduring interest in exploring a cluster of schemas: trajectory, transporting, containing and enveloping.

- Caitlin's reactions to changes, fears and loss.

EXPLORING A CLUSTER OF SCHEMAS: TRAJECTORY, TRANSPORTING, CONTAINING AND ENVELOPING

Observation: Caitlin and her friend <u>envelop</u> with paint and water

Caitlin (2:06:28) and Lee were alongside each other at the easel. Each child had a paintbrush and was painting their own hand before holding them up to show each other. Caitlin asked Colette, the adult filming, 'I want my sleeves up'. She held both hands up and Colette said 'Your hands are covered in paint …

And yours, Lee'. Caitlin rubbed her hands against each other and held them up again. Colette said 'Purple and blue hands!' Caitlin rubbed them again. Colette 'What does it feel like? Does it feel nice?'

Caitlin stepped off the block she was standing on and went towards the bathroom. Colette 'You're washing your hands?' Lee followed a second later. Colette 'You're washing yours as well mate'.

In the bathroom, Caitlin grinned as she put each of her hands under a tap. She stopped and pushed her sleeves up and laughed at Lee, washing his hands at the adjacent sink.

Colette 'You're making the water all purple, Lee' and to Caitlin 'And you're making it all blue'.

Caitlin stopped and used the soap dispenser to put some soap on one hand before washing them again. She picked up a wet paper towel from the back of the sink and wiped the soap dispenser, then she held the paper towel under the dispenser and put soap onto the wet towel. She then wiped the outside of the soap dispenser with the wet, soapy towel and Lee joined in, wiping the dispenser with a wet paper towel too.

DISCUSSION AND INTERPRETATION OF CAITLIN AND LEE'S ACTIONS AND COMMUNICATION

Using schema theory to interpret Caitlin's actions showed that Caitlin was 'covering' or 'enveloping' her hands with paint (Athey, 1990, p. 149). She transformed them from skin colour to blue. Athey (1990, p. 152) stated that 'Almost all the children represented "darkness" as well as envelopment by scribbling over or covering over, their drawings'. Caitlin gave no indication of what she was representing by covering her hands with paint. She was also discovering the properties of the paint. When spread thinly on a surface, it quickly dried. She was rubbing her hands together and very soon feeling the dryness. Arnold (1999, p. 107) studied Georgia who systematically explored 'whether liquids dry when sprinkled or spread thinly'.

Caitlin was also interested in enveloping her hands with water and soap. She discovered that removing the paint from her hands was 'functionally dependent' on wetting her hands and rubbing soap on (Athey, 1990, p. 69). Caitlin may also have been interested in the transformation of the water from transparent to translucent blue. Her subsequent 'washing' of the soap dispenser indicated that she was repeating her enveloping pattern with different materials and on different surfaces.

With regard to emotions, Caitlin was probably just enjoying the feel of covering her hands with paint. Both covering with thick liquid (for example, paint) and washing with water, was probably soothing. Although Caitlin did not respond to Colette's question 'How does it feel?' she was obviously enjoying the feel of painting her hands and rubbing them together while the paint was wet. As soon as the paint dried she went to the bathroom to wash her hands and to, once again, experience the feel of the liquid on her hands. Caitlin also seemed to be identifying with Lee and enjoyed carrying out the same actions as him.

Almost every time Caitlin was observed, she placed materials in containers (buttons in a box, water in bottles, sand in bowls). The following observation was typical of Caitlin's explorations at this time.

Observation: Caitlin filling containers with water and placing them in a line

At 2:09:22 Caitlin was at the sink filling jugs with water. She walked to the water tray nearby and picked up a small plant pot, looked down at the adult-sized pink shoes she was wearing and at the adult's shoes.

Caitlin *'I got some … shoes'.*

Colette *(adult) 'You've got lovely pink shoes'.*

Caitlin *'And you've got …' (pointing down at Colette's shoes).*

Colette *'I've got brown shoes on today'.*

Caitlin went to the sink and tried to fill the plant pot with water from the tap but it ran through the holes in the base. She picked up a large spoon and tried to put it into a bottle but found it did not fit. Caitlin bent down and selected some bottles from a basket saying 'I got three'. She picked up several more bottles and filled each of them with water before placing them at the back of the sink. She needed help to lift the largest bottle, when it was full of water. She filled the space available.

Then Caitlin took a jug from her 'line' of containers to the bathroom and filled it with water. After emptying the water out, she put soap in the bottom of the jug from the soap dispenser. She added water from the tap which created bubbles on the surface of the water. She repeated this and talked about making 'coffee'.

DISCUSSION AND INTERPRETATION OF CAITLIN'S ACTIONS AND COMMUNICATION

Using schema theory indicates that Caitlin was assimilating new materials into her <u>containing</u> pattern. She showed an interest in the shoes that were <u>containers</u> for her feet. When she tried to <u>contain</u> water in a plant pot, she had to accommodate to the idea that the water ran through the holes in the base of her container. She rejected the plant pot and therefore it could be said that she was not ready to accommodate to the new 'going through a boundary' pattern or to use it in her play at this time.

Caitlin also discovered that she could not put a large spoon into a narrow-necked container as it did not fit. After trying to contain water in a plant pot and a spoon in a bottle, she selected several containers (bottles and jugs) and filled each of them with water. She placed the containers full of water in close proximity to each other, at the back of the sink. Caitlin not only filled the containers with water, but also filled the available space with a line of full containers. The line had end points and, as Athey (1990, p. 155) has pointed out, the containers sub-divided the space, heralding later understanding of measuring and counting.

When we use attachment theory to understand Caitlin's actions, we can draw on the spatial aspect of placing the full containers 'in close proximity' to each other. Although this seems a tenuous link, Caitlin seemed satisfied that the containers were close and touching each other so she may have been repre-senting proximity or connection with the containers.

Caitlin seemed to derive some satisfaction from filling the containers, as well as placing them next to each other. 'Having' lots of containers, as well filling them with lots of water seemed important to Caitlin.

Her conversation was about what she had 'got', for example pink shoes, three bottles. When she went into the bathroom and put soap into a jug and then filled it with water, Caitlin told us she was representing 'coffee'. Her mum drank coffee at home so the representation of coffee may also have repre-sented 'having' what her mum had and, therefore, made her feel more powerful and also connected her to her mum.

Caitlin's enduring motive seemed to be possession. Containing materials or objects enabled Caitlin to carry them about, keep them together and exert and display her power over them. This is a common motive in young children. Susan Isaacs (1933, p. 221) pointed out 'the common wish of little children to have exclusive possession or at least the biggest share or main use of what-ever properties are the centre of interest at the moment'.

I have really struggled to understand Caitlin's actions, particularly when thinking about links with her emotional world. Her desire to contain and keep together whatever she was using is a behaviour I strongly identify with, even as an adult. I think the root, for me, of those repeated behaviours is sib-ling rivalry and the desire to have as much or more than my siblings.

Isaacs (1933, p. 232) linked rivalry with 'the family situation' in which chil-dren are rivals 'for the love of adults, and primarily, of course, the parents'. So the gathering of materials might be linked to personal worth. 'Having' lots might be a symbol of needing lots of love and also of being worth lots of love.

In Caitlin's case, she derived satisfaction from this gathering. Isaacs said that little children are so dependent 'on the love and care of adults that they have an absolute need to possess them and their love'. Caitlin's brother was very demanding at this time and, although she would blame him for things even when he was not there, her mother said that generally the two children got on well. Caitlin may have learned some of her strategies from her experiences with her brother at home. Perhaps her need to 'gather' things was because her brother 'gathered' a disproportionate amount of attention from her mum.

Caitlin continued to enjoy filling containers and lining them up. One day, when Caitlin was 3 years, 1 month and 29 days, she and her friend, Lee, used hoses to fill 15 buckets with water in the Beach Area. She worked closely with her friend to refill the buckets when a boy knocked five of them over. Caitlin defended her friend when another child came close, demonstrating her assertiveness.

CAITLIN'S REACTIONS TO CHANGES, FEARS AND LOSS

CONTEXT

During her first year at nursery, Caitlin's life was fairly stable. She lived with her mum, brother and mum's partner, made a close relationship with her Family Worker at nursery, Danielle, and also developed a close friendship with Lee.

However, during Caitlin's second year, some things changed for her, both at home and at nursery. In this section, I am presenting observations that link with Caitlin's responses to those changes.

The first major change was in October 2003 when Caitlin's mum's partner moved out of the family home. This caused distress for Caitlin's mother and for both children. The following video observation shows Caitlin engaging in play that was less characteristic of her. Instead of seeking out her friends, Lee or Morgan, she went to the computer.

Observation: At the computer

I had just arrived and asked Caitlin how her mum was.

Caitlin *'She buyed me a bike'. Caitlin (3:02:23) then ran and sat at a computer in the corridor, alongside Connie, who was being settled in by her dad. Caitlin manipulated the mouse, pressed her computer screen, looked towards nursery and said 'Lee' but did not move.*

Caitlin made several attempts to interact with Connie:

Caitlin smiled at Connie, leaned across and touched Connie's screen. Then she pressed her own screen and said 'Connie, look!' Both children laughed. Caitlin continued to use her computer, then leaned across and turned Connie's mouse around. Caitlin leaned down and got a CD out of a box under the table.

Connie's dad moved away for a couple of minutes. Caitlin leaned across and pressed the button to release the CD drawer from Connie's computer, then took Connie's CD out and put it into the box under the table. She then leaned across and put another CD into Connie's CD drawer and pressed the button to make it retract.

Connie's dad came back. Caitlin leaned across and said 'Connie, you don't put ...' Connie said 'I do it'. Then Caitlin leaned across and pulled Connie's keyboard out saying 'Connie, do these ones', then pulled her own keyboard out and pressed some buttons.

Caitlin watched the 'goodbye':

Connie's dad ejected her CD and went to get another one. Connie said 'Daddy put it away' pointing to the empty drawer. Connie's dad put another CD in, kissed her 'Goodbye' and left. Caitlin watched as he left. Caitlin got up and went to a nearby table, which was set up with make up and mirrors. She picked up two make-up bags and went back and gave one to Connie...

DISCUSSION AND INTERPRETATION OF CAITLIN'S ACTIONS AND COMMUNICATION

Using schema theory to understand Caitlin's actions, Caitlin used a '<u>dab</u>' or '<u>trajectory</u>' movement to press the screen, button and also the keyboard. She was very interested in taking the CD out and putting it back into the drawer, thereby <u>containing</u> it. She continued after Connie left and later on in this observation, to repeatedly take CDs out of the drawer and replace them. She had no interest in actually playing them. I think she was interested in the functional dependency aspect, that is, the CD drawer coming out and going in was functionally dependent on pressing the button. She was, therefore, co-ordinating <u>trajectory</u> and <u>containing</u> schemas. Caitlin chose two bags from the make-up table, again <u>containers</u>.

Using attachment theory to understand Caitlin's interactions, here Caitlin began by telling me what her mum had bought her, a new bike, and was therefore about 'having' and worth. Caitlin had an opportunity to watch Connie's relationship with her dad at close quarters. She watched the actual separation quite closely. However, most of her energy went into trying to <u>connect</u> with Connie. She tried to assist Connie with her computer, but Connie did not really want her assistance and she had her dad there to help anyway. Caitlin suggested that they both used their keyboards but Connie did not take this up. Finally Caitlin fetched two make-up bags so they both had <u>containers</u>. Did Caitlin think that Connie might need a container as her dad had left?

I wonder whether Caitlin wanted to feel more powerful and if her way of feeling powerful was to be able to help other children with 'doing' things. The other way of connecting was to 'have' the same as each other and she tried this strategy with the make-up bags.

Caitlin saw Lee arrive but did not go and join him. One possible explanation for why Caitlin chose to be at the computer in the corridor and to stay there on that morning, was that it was the area where Danielle (her Family Worker) was placed that week. If Caitlin was feeling vulnerable, it may have helped to be near Danielle.

Observation: Asking Danielle for cuddles

… Danielle walked past and Caitlin left the computer, carrying the make-up bag, and put both arms up to Danielle. Danielle lifted her up and held her and kissed her. Caitlin's arms went floppy. Danielle said, 'Can I set these chairs out?' and put Caitlin down while she set some chairs near the make-up table. Caitlin manipulated a plastic hair clasp, that was on the table.

Caitlin picked up a brush and comb, moved over to Danielle and held her arms up again. Danielle crouched down and held Caitlin again, while greeting Susan.

Caitlin *said 'My mum says where's her jacket?'*

Danielle *replied 'Where's her jacket … she found it though, 'cos she was wearing a coat'*

Caitlin *said 'In the cupboard' smiling.*

DISCUSSION AND INTERPRETATION OF CAITLIN'S ACTIONS AND COMMUNICATION

Using schema theory to understand, Caitlin 'transported' the make-up bag when she approached Danielle. Then she 'transported' a brush and comb from the make-up table when she approached Danielle for a second time. These could have been 'objects of transition' from one area to another, or something to talk about when approaching someone or objects that represented her interests (Bruce, 2004).

Using attachment theory to understand, Caitlin expressed her wish to be near Danielle and to be held by her. Her arms went floppy when Danielle first held her, possibly showing her complete trust in Danielle's ability to 'contain' her feelings.

Susan was a younger child, fairly new to nursery at this time and also in Danielle's group. Caitlin may have seen Susan as a rival for Danielle's affection. Although Caitlin did not show any hostility towards Susan, she did show that she needed Danielle, so she was 'in touch with' her 'wishes, needs, feelings, thoughts' (Laevers, 1997, p. 19).

Caitlin's comment about her mum's jacket may have been significant too. It showed that she was thinking about her mum and, although she did not mention the greater loss, she mentioned the fact that her mum had lost her jacket but then found it in a cupboard.

OTHER CHANGES

During the next few weeks, Caitlin's great granny was very ill and her granny also became ill. Danielle, her Family Worker, was off work because of her pregnancy.

Observation: Caitlin and Lee sweeping the surface of water in the barrel

Caitlin (3:04:00) and Lee were sweeping the surface of the water in the barrel in the Discovery Area. Suddenly Caitlin said to me 'My granny's birthday now'. I said 'Is it?' Caitlin said 'Again'. Then she said to Lee 'Not yours'.

DISCUSSION AND INTERPRETATION OF CAITLIN'S ACTIONS AND COMMUNICATION

I wonder whether sweeping with a broom brought Caitlin's granny to mind or whether she was on her mind anyway. Using schema theory to understand, Caitlin may have been beginning to understand that birthdays come around every year for everyone. Perhaps she could remember her granny's last birthday? So calendars and time could be thought about as circular rather than linear (<u>rotating</u> rather than a <u>trajectory</u>).

Using attachment theory to understand, this short sequence indicated that Caitlin was thinking about her granny and feeling possessive about her Granny's birthday. Susan Isaacs (1933, p. 222) described how two children in her study, 'Harold and Paul[,] felt a keen sense of property in the nursery rhymes and songs they had heard at home'. Caitlin's was a similar kind of claim. Usually she was keen to share but, in this case, she needed to think about '**her** granny's birthday' and could not share that with Lee.

When someone is on your mind because they are ill or needy in some way, it can preoccupy you and make it difficult to become involved in the usual way. I would not judge Caitlin to be completely preoccupied with her granny, but she was thinking about her and was needing to exert her power in claiming her 'granny's birthday' more strongly than she usually did.

Observation: Cuddle with Angela

Three days later, Caitlin sought out Angela (Head of Nursery):

Angela's first day back after two weeks in America. Danielle has been off sick. Caitlin came for a cuddle with Angela while we were talking. Caitlin talked about 'fireworks being loud' and waking her up at night. She also said she saw a car set on fire. She enjoyed sitting with Angela.

Four days later, Caitlin had a conversation with me:

Caitlin said 'I'm not frightened of bogeymen'.

I said 'There's no such thing'.

Caitlin replied 'When you put the lights out …'.

Later that day:

Caitlin said 'Snake – Lorna's got a snake – bite you, eat you. Lee's scared of snakes …'.

DISCUSSION AND INTERPRETATION OF CAITLIN'S ACTIONS AND COMMUNICATION

Using schema theory, these observations indicate that, for Caitlin, when the world is covered or <u>enveloped</u> by darkness, then every sound is more frightening. The snake conversation may have revealed a fear of being 'eaten up' or 'engulfed' by another creature.

Using attachment theory, Caitlin was talking about bedtime as a scary time, when the lights were out and her mum was not close to her. Bowlby (1998, pp. 132–47) drew on several studies of young children, both in naturalistic and experimental situations, to deduce that certain universal situations provoke fear in children under 5. He also noted that 'compound situations', for example, 'being alone, in darkness and hearing a sudden sound' would provoke fear in most people, not just young children (1998, p. 147). Leaving aside the fear of separation, Bowlby (1998, p. 141) found the universal fear provoking situations, in relation to young children, were 'noise … strange people … animals … and, darkness'.

In my discussions with Caitlin's mother, she said that Caitlin had started to be more fearful since she had 'got her off the dummy'. She reported that Caitlin would say there was 'a monster under the bed'. Anna would check and reassure her there was no monster and would also leave the hall light on.

We also discussed the fact that Caitlin's great granny had been diagnosed with throat cancer. I asked whether Caitlin knew how ill she was and Anna felt it was not right to 'tell a little child', though undoubtedly, Caitlin was picking up on her mother's anxieties at this time.

This took me right back to my own early belief that, as a parent, I could protect my children from pain. I am aware that I still do not know the best way to face up to a situation like the impending death of a close relative. I imagine that Anna is quite open with Caitlin and her brother usually, but that this was a new situation for her. She had thought about what to say to Caitlin and did not feel that it was right to burden (?) her with this knowledge.

Caitlin had already experienced the loss of her dummy and of her stepfather. I know that Caitlin could ask her mum questions and that she had a good understanding of the family situation, as Anna had told me that when her stepdad was telling her off she would say to him 'You're not my real dad'. Caitlin also asked whether her mum liked him once he had left. She told Caitlin that she did not like him any more.

MORE CHANGES AFTER CHRISTMAS

CONTEXT

There was a gap in the observations over Christmas and while I went away on holiday.

On my first day back to lunch Danielle told me that Caitlin's great granny had died and that her granny had been diagnosed with stomach cancer.

Three days later I filmed Caitlin outside in the Beach Area with Louise (adult). Louise said it had been quite difficult to engage Caitlin that day as she seemed to be feeling low.

Observation: Caitlin and Louise filling containers with sand

Caitlin (3:07:22) filled several containers (bowls, buckets and bun tins) with sand. She encouraged Louise (adult) to join in. Caitlin wanted to have the same as Louise had. For example, when Caitlin noticed that the crate Louise was sitting on was a slightly different green to hers, she swapped hers for an identical one and said 'It's the same green'.

Louise noticed that Caitlin's crate was the right way up whereas Louise's was upside down, so Caitlin was sitting inside the crate.

Louise asked 'Are you all right sitting like that? I've turned my crate round the other way, like that'.

Caitlin stood up and said 'You do it to mine'. Louise turned it over and Caitlin sat down.

Louise asked 'Does that feel more comfortable?'

Caitlin said 'Yes' ...

Louise suggested 'You've nearly finished?' and asked 'What are you making?' Caitlin responded 'I know, we can cook it in there' (pointing to some hollow blocks).

Louise said 'Do we need to find a little oven?' Caitlin moved around finding more buckets and pans.

Louise asked 'Are we doing lots of baking then?'

Caitlin 'Yes' ...

DISCUSSION AND INTERPRETATION OF CAITLIN'S ACTIONS AND COMMUNICATION

Using schema theory to understand, Caitlin seemed very focused on finding <u>containers</u> and <u>filling</u> them with sand. Towards the end of this sequence, she was thinking about putting her containers of sand <u>inside</u> another container. Like Brenda in Athey's study (1990, p. 150) Caitlin was using her <u>containing</u> schema at a symbolic representational level when she talked about 'cooking it in there'.

Another schematic interest seemed to be <u>classification</u> in the sense of wanting to have the same as Louise and do the same as Louise. Athey (1990, p. 41) stated that '*classification* has its origins in early actions applied to a wide range of objects and, later, to events'. Caitlin needed to be able to recognise similarities and differences in order to apply a classification to objects and actions.

Using attachment theory, Caitlin seemed to be using her play to engage with Louise. Both were trying to engender shared interest. Caitlin's motive seemed to be to have Louise to herself and to stay in close proximity to Louise. Louise was keen for Caitlin to become deeply involved and for her well-being to become higher. We saw in earlier observations that Caitlin seemed to gain strength from her solidarity with others. Louise 'tuned in' to Caitlin's need to be the same by noticing that Caitlin's crate was a different way up and pointing that out to her.

Thinking about the language each of them used, they began by talking about 'you' and 'me' or 'mine'. Caitlin introduced 'we' and then this was taken up by Louise, who retorted 'Do we need ...?' Was this the point at which the game became a joint venture?

For me, as a practitioner, one of the big questions is whether to comment on a child's lower well-being to them. Does that help or merely confirm what they are feeling? Is it helpful to have your feelings confirmed by another person? Marrone with Diamond (1998, p. 149) drew on Bowlby's research and concluded that 'Disconfirmation of the child's perception and knowledge often leads to permanent cognitive disturbance and other problems, such as chronic distrust of other people, inhibition of their curiosity, distrust of their own senses and a tendency to find everything unreal'.

This raises the question of whether we disconfirm a child's feelings by ignoring or avoiding how they are feeling? Elfer (1996, p. 34) when working with nursery nurses, who had used distraction as a strategy to deal with children's distress at separation, found that the nursery nurses realised that 'there were benefits in picking them up and allowing them to have "a good cry"'. The staff found that after a good cry, some children 'settled down to play'.

Thinking about Caitlin's actions of <u>containing</u> sand, Winnicott (1991, p. 46) described a child's play of <u>containing</u> small toys in pockets and other containers, as 'of a self-healing kind'. It is much easier to recognise children's projections onto small world figures or soft toys than it is to make links between their actions with materials such as sand and water. Again, Caitlin wanted to 'have' lots, both for herself and her chosen play partner, Louise.

Another way of acknowledging Caitlin's feelings was to accept and be open to what she chose to say and do. It was certainly no coincidence that she chose to be near and to interact with Louise that day. We had noticed, in an earlier study, that children were drawn to adults, who could meet their particular emotional or cognitive needs (Arnold, 2004) and that some adults were focused more strongly on the emotional domain and some were focused more strongly on the cognitive domain. Louise was clearly interested in emotions and open to receiving and containing Caitlin's emotions.

Caitlin continued to explore <u>containing</u> and <u>enveloping</u> throughout this period and, if there was a change, it was that 'having' sometimes became more important than 'doing'. During the sequence in the sand with Louise, Caitlin surrounded herself with containers, which she filled. They could be seen as a protective layer, between her and the rest of the world, surrounding or <u>enclosing</u> her and her play partner. <u>Filling</u> so many containers also kept her very busy and engaged with Louise. Again she gained some satisfaction from having and filling lots, which may come back to being worth lots.

Observation: Knowing how to seek comfort

Danielle says that Caitlin has been feeling low because of recent events. Caitlin said to Danielle 'I know what – I'll go and get a blanket and you can wrap it around me and hold me like a dolly'. Danielle was amazed that Caitlin knew that she wanted to be held and contained, that it would help and that she was able to articulate her need.

Danielle had frequent and unpredictable absences at this time, because of her pregnancy.

Louise reported that Caitlin (3:08:18) had become close to her recently.

DISCUSSION AND INTERPRETATION OF CAITLIN'S ACTIONS AND COMMUNICATION

Using schema theory to understand Caitlin's actions, her wish to be held and <u>contained</u> in a blanket in Danielle's arms was not surprising. I wondered whether this was something she had experienced her mother doing when she was in distress.

Using attachment theory, Caitlin was able to express her need to be near and to be held by Danielle. In Danielle's absence, she had become close to Louise, another gentle person, who was open to hearing children's emotional needs.

Caitlin had a great ability to simply say what she wanted. In my experience, this ability is rare, even in adults. She seemed to intuitively know that her strength came from being with other people, being 'we' rather than 'I'. When she was most vulnerable, she drew on the skills of sensitive adults to support her.

Although Caitlin and her family had a fairly difficult year, in terms of loss and change, Caitlin still seemed to come through as emotionally competent. She had resources to draw on, which could be described as 'emotional capital' (Reay, 2002). Her relationship with her mother was very open. Her mother described her as quite mischievous and a boundary pusher, but with a keen sense of humour. Her mother frequently used humour to cope with adversity and this may be the key. Music (2004, p. 31) reported that 'parents who could be playfully in touch with, but not feel overly threatened by, their infants' emotions' helped their infants to recover quickly. When we saw Caitlin on video falling over and getting up and carrying on with her game, her mother commented that at home, she would say 'Rub it and laugh because you're going to end up with something much worse when you are older'. Her mother could offer comfort but also distance in her comments. This is different to pure distraction when adults could be denying or not acknowledging a child's pain.

SO WHAT?

We learned a great deal from observing Caitlin and from our dialogue with Anna. Although we cannot claim that Caitlin was prompted to use <u>enveloping</u> and <u>containing</u> because of her emotional need at the time, it was interesting to see how she used her interest in <u>containing</u> to create a boundary between her and Louise and other children. She also seemed to have a clear understanding of how Danielle could 'hold' her in order to comfort her and contain her feelings.

In order to generalise our learning to other children, we realised that, as workers, it was critical to:

- Know about important events at home, such as separations, illness and whatever was causing anxiety in families.

- Comfort and support children in the way they want when necessary.

- Notice different behaviours in children – one way of doing this was to monitor 'well-being' in children on a regular basis (Laevers, 1997).

- Be clear about how, as workers, we deal with children's distress and anxiety.

- Have a support and supervision system in place whereby the distress of workers could be identified, discussed and contained. Research has shown that sometimes workers are unaware of the 'emotional labour' they experience which leaves them exhausted and physically and emotionally worn out.

Table 4.1 Schemas mentioned and links made

Containing	Caitlin put various materials into different containers. These actions seemed to represent 'having' lots and being worth lots; Caitlin wanted to be 'contained' and held in a blanket
Enveloping	Caitlin enveloped her hands in paint. She seemed to like the feel of this
Transporting	Caitlin brought things from home and was very skilled at acquiring high status objects another child might want to share. This seemed to give Caitlin a strategy for connecting with others
Trajectory	Pressing the button in order to make the CD drawer go inside seemed to fascinate Caitlin
Going through a boundary	Caitlin seemed to reject the 'going through' function of a plant pot with holes in the bottom when she wanted something that would hold water inside
Proximity	Caitlin placed bottles of water next to each other

Table 4.1

Connection	Caitlin arranged bottles of water so that each touched the next
Dab	Dab was a technique for opening the CD drawer which Caitlin seemed to find satisfying. She also used a dab movement to play on a touch-screen computer
Filling	Caitlin filled containers right to the top. This action may have signified 'having' as much as possible, e.g. water, sand
Classification	Sorting objects so that she and a play partner had the same seemed to make Caitlin feel powerful
Enclosing	Caitlin seemed to use buckets of sand to enclose and protect her and her play partner

SUGGESTED FURTHER READING

Arnold, C. (1999) *Child Development and Learning 2–5 years: Georgia's Story*, Paul Chapman, London.

Athey, C. (1990) *Extending Thought in Young Children*, Paul Chapman, London.

Athey, C. (2007) *Extending Thought in Young Children*, 2nd edn, Paul Chapman, London.

Isaacs, S. (1933) *Social Development in Young Children*, George Routledge and Sons, London.

Laevers, F. (1997) *A Process-Oriented Child Follow-up System for Young Children*, Centre for Experiential Education, Leuven University, Belgium.

Edward: Exploring 'Together' and 'Apart' and Moving from 'Vertical' to 'Horizontal' with Objects

This chapter introduces:

- Edward and his family

- An observation of Edward's painful separation from his mother at nursery and his subsequent actions

- Other observations of Edward exploring 'together' and 'apart'

- Observations of Edward exploring 'vertical' to 'horizontal'

INTRODUCTION AND CONTEXT

Edward was 2 years 9 months and in his first year at nursery when I made my first observation of him. Edward is the youngest of three children. He has two older sisters. For the previous two years Edward had come into nursery, almost daily, in his buggy with his mum, who was bringing his sister to attend the nursery. So he was very familiar with the setting and the people. In his second year at Pen Green Nursery, Edward attended four full days each week. At nursery and at home, Edward had a strong and enduring interest in 'connecting' and 'disconnecting'. I have chosen to present some video sequences that exemplify this and also his later interest in moving from a vertical to a horizontal position, that enabled us to raise questions about a possible link between Edward's actions and his emotional world.

Edward had had some difficulty settling at nursery and separating from his mother, Janet. His Family Worker, Annette, had been working on using and extending his interest in phones to help him settle at nursery each day. Having his mum's mobile phone seemed to help Edward in two ways: he knew she had entrusted him with something precious of hers and, ultimately, he could ring her and gain reassurance from her about where she was or when she was coming back for him.

Two of the themes that emerged from observing Edward were:

- His interest in <u>connecting</u> and <u>disconnecting.</u>

- His exploration of <u>vertical</u> to <u>horizontal.</u>

CONNECTING AND DISCONNECTING

Observation: The separation

Edward (2:9:00) was filmed coming into the building, looking anxious, frowning and staying very close to his mum, pressing his body against her legs. When it came to the actual separation, Janet too, looked anxious and left after telling him she had to go and saying a quick goodbye. Edward became very distressed, ran after his mum and, when he realised she had gone, lay down on the floor near the exit and cried. Annette stroked his back but he wriggled away from her and would not allow her to comfort him at first.

She stayed nearby and, after a couple of minutes, he allowed Annette to rub his back and to lift him up. She put him down in the cloakroom nearby, thinking he would need his coat on to go outside but he said 'No' to going outside. She lifted him up and carried him on her hip down the corridor towards the main nursery room.

Annette tried to engage Edward by offering him choices. Did he want to go outside? Or on the computer? He shook his head but then pointed at the hook hanging undone at the top of the men's toilet door. Annette carried him near to it. He fastened the hook. Annette pointed to the bathroom door, which had a similar hook and eye. She carried him close to it. He unhooked it and then fastened it and smiled. Annette looked around and said 'Trevor's office?' The hook was undone. Edward did it up and smiled again. Annette carried Edward into the main nursery room and said 'I think Maureen (the cleaner) might have one'. Annette carried Edward to the laundry room door. He unhooked the hook, fastened it, unhooked it and fastened it again, smiling.

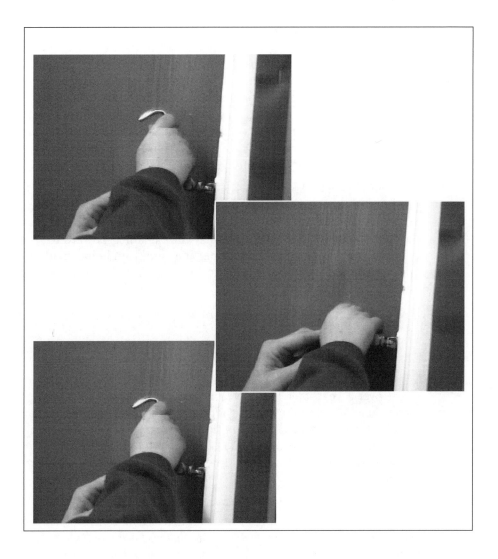

DISCUSSION AND INTERPRETATION OF EDWARD'S ACTIONS AND COMMUNICATION

I watched this sequence many times alongside Edward's mother, his Family Worker and other colleagues. In terms of schemas, Edward was using a 'going through a boundary' schema in order to 'connect' the hook to the eye (Athey, 1990, pp. 156 and p. 87).

In terms of attachment, what may have been significant to him at first, was a hook hanging undone (or disconnected) while he was feeling the pain of being separated (or disconnected) from his mother. He certainly noticed the unconnected hook and derived some pleasure and satisfaction from reconnecting it.

Each time Edward 'connected' a hook to an eye, he looked pleased and satisfied. Through unfastening and fastening each hook, he was learning about the function of a hook and eye, and about proximity and separation. His actions may also have been helping him to begin to work through and understand his own feelings about being separated and also helping him to gain some level of control in this situation, just as the children cited by Susan Isaacs did. He seemed to be representing 'together' and 'apart' and was most satisfied with 'together'. Could this have been a sort of 'transitional' behavior, symbolising and giving form to his separation from his mum?

Through engaging Annette in his game, he was physically 'held' for several minutes while they went around the different doors (Winnicott, 2006). Edward seemed angry with Annette at first for separating him from his mother. The game that developed may have enabled Edward to receive some comfort or healing both from 'connecting' and from being 'held' in Annette's arms to connect. Annette seemed to understand his need to receive comfort and to comfort himself in this way.

Edward continued to be interested in any objects he could take apart.

Observation: Edward playing with a Hoover

Just over a year later I observed Edward playing in the nursery. He had continued to be interested in gadgets, particularly anything he could take apart. He was so intent on taking things apart at home that the family 'had been through four mobile phones and a stereo'. He was still sometimes distressed at separation times.

Edward (3:9:16) had continued to enjoy gadgets and phones. On this occasion, Edward was playing with an old Hoover, brought in by Katey (a worker) in order to extend his understanding of how machines work. Edward spent some time with another boy, John. Some of the morning was spent taking the container for dust and filter off the Hoover and trying to fit them back on. Then he and John took the Hoover outside …

… They dragged the Hoover indoors, across the nursery and back to the lobby. Edward took two wheels off the bottom of the Hoover and struggled to put them back on. When he had managed to fix them back on, he showed his satisfaction by saying 'That's the idea!' and then repeated his sequence of actions several times.

He asked me for his 'robot' (he meant dust container) and tried to fix it back onto the Hoover. He said 'I need to fix it for Katey – she's gonna take it home' and then (to me) 'Will you fix it?'

DISCUSSION AND INTERPRETATION OF EDWARD'S ACTIONS AND COMMUNICATION

In schema terms, Edward again spent some of the time 'disconnecting' and 'connecting' parts of the Hoover. He showed satisfaction, both in his body language and spoken language, when he managed to 'connect' or fix bits of the Hoover back together. He repeated the process of 'taking apart' and 'fitting together' several times. He may have been interested in 'reversibility' and whether **he** could 'fix' the Hoover (Athey, 1990, p. 41). His final query suggested that he thought I could fix the hoover.

In attachment terms, we speculated whether these explorations mirrored his explorations of separation and reunion in his relationships? Was he repeating his actions in order to represent 'together' and 'apart' in his relationships? Was he trying to demonstrate that he could be separated and come back together and feel part of a coherent whole?

Observation: Edward trying to fix a helmet

Edward (3:9:30) went to the writing area and selected a roll of masking tape and some scissors. He cut some tape and then ran with it to the main nursery room. He picked up a plastic helmet with a visor, which was hanging off at one side. He handed the visor to Angela (adult), who held it, while Edward placed tape on, to try to repair the visor. Edward spent the next few minutes cutting pieces of tape and putting them on the visor in an effort to repair it. Each time he placed more tape on, he moved the visor and the tape loosened. He said something about 'going to the shop to fix it'. Angela said 'You're like Bob the Builder, a fixer, aren't you?'

Edward placed several pieces of tape on the visor. Then he cut a very long piece of tape and wrapped it around, enclosing the whole helmet. Angela demonstrated that it would not go on her head with tape underneath. He ripped the tape off.

DISCUSSION AND INTERPRETATION OF EDWARD'S ACTIONS AND COMMUNICATION

This sequence showed Edward, once more, in schema terms, engaged in 'connecting' or fixing something that had come apart or separated (Athey, 1990). He experimented with doing this in different ways, by bridging a gap and by 'enclosing' the whole helmet. In this instance, retaining flexibility was important for the visor to be able to move from the vertical to the horizontal.

This was a more complex process than placing an eye through a hook or fitting wheels back onto the hoover.

In attachment terms, Edward was intent once more in making something whole or making the helmet and visor <u>connect</u> and work together. Here was something that had broken and Edward seemed to have a strong resolve to try in different ways to fix it. In this instance, he did not succeed but seemed to show some persistence and resilience in his efforts to repair the helmet (Kraemer, 2000).

Edward continued spending a lot of his time '<u>connecting</u>' or fixing objects. He became the boy who raced to answer the phone whenever it rang in the nursery, again demonstrating his interest in making connections in different ways.

Another machine that fascinated Edward was the street-cleaning lorry. One day I observed him struggling to carry the heavy doormats from the nursery into the cloakroom. He seemed to be playing at 'cleaning'.

Observation: Edward cleaning

Edward (4:0:6) went into the cloakroom and bent down and systematically rolled up a heavy rubber-backed mat and placed it in one corner, leaning it against the wall …

Edward went over to the rolled-up mat, carried it and leant it against a different corner of the room. Then he knelt down and systematically rolled the second mat up. Edward placed the second rolled-up mat with the first, leaning into one corner in the cloakroom.

(In between this heavy work, he swept the floor with a big broom – see the next observation.)

Edward dragged one mat towards the doorway into the nursery, dropped it on the floor and unfolded it … he fetched the second mat and unrolled it by standing at one end and holding the edge of the mat so that it unrolled. He spent some time lining the two mats up, edge to edge on the floor and overlapping the edge of one precisely and neatly over the edge of the second. When he was satisfied, he stood up and walked away, raising his arms slightly and sighing in what Trevarthen and then Tait have described as a 'chuffed' manner' (Trevarthen, 2003; Tait, 2004, 2005).

DISCUSSION AND INTERPRETATION OF EDWARD'S ACTIONS AND COMMUNICATION

One action immediately struck me as significant in Edward's exploration of cleaning:

- His arrangement of the mats so that there was a perfect overlap and his obvious satisfaction with that arrangement.

In terms of schema theory, this part of Edward's exploration was leading towards tessellation (Athey, 2003). He 'connected' the mats perfectly, resulting in a larger area of the floor being covered or 'enveloped' by the two mats acting as one.

In terms of 'attachment', here was a perfectly seamless connection between the two mats. He showed his satisfaction with this 'perfect' arrangement by looking 'chuffed' with himself.

Another persistent concern of Edward's was with the movement from vertical to horizontal.

VERTICAL TO HORIZONTAL

Observation: Other aspects of Edward cleaning

Edward (4:0:6) went into the cloakroom and bent down and systematically rolled up a heavy rubber-backed mat and placed it in one corner, leaning against the wall …

Edward bent down and picked up a large broom. He swept with the broom in front of him … then moved away and leaned the broom against the central pillar. He covered his ears as it fell over (anticipating that it would fall?).

Edward went over to the rolled-up mat, carried it and leaned it against a different corner of the room. Then he knelt down and systematically rolled the second mat up … Edward placed the second rolled-up mat with the first, leaning into one corner in the cloakroom …

Edward picked up the broom and swept the mats.

Then he dropped the broom and kicked it under a nearby seat.

He knelt down near the mats and asked me to turn the camera around so that he could see himself, then rolled up the first mat, carried it, then dropped it and kicked it under the seat …

He fetched the mop and bucket from nursery and began mopping the cloakroom floor … Edward became machine like, leaning on the end of the mop handle and moving forward with the mop in front of him. He chased me playfully, saying 'I will clean you up' twice.

Edward went into the nursery, tried to lean the mop against a cupboard and dropped it when it did not lean.

DISCUSSION AND INTERPRETATION OF EDWARD'S ACTIONS AND COMMUNICATION

Edward was intent on rolling up each mat and leaning the rolled-up mats against the wall. This was no mean feat as they were quite heavy and unwieldy. He put a lot of effort into trying to achieve his aim.

In terms of schema theory, Edward was transforming the appearance of materials through his actions. He transformed the mats from a two-dimensional form to a three-dimensional form. Furthermore, being able to lean the mats against the wall was 'functionally dependent' on Edward rolling them up tightly first (Athey, 1990, p. 69) and in placing them at an angle in a place that would '<u>enclose</u>' or '<u>contain</u>' them, the corner of the cloakroom.

He went from leaning the mats at an angle to using his own body with the broom handle to create a similar <u>oblique</u> effect. Later on, he used the mop in a similar way. He leaned his body against the end of the mop handle and pushed it so that it moved forward like a machine. Edward seemed to be exploring:

- Using his body as a force to set something in motion.

- Using his body as a force to keep the object at a consistent <u>oblique</u> angle.

- Different amounts of friction as properties of a brush and mop on the same surface.

When he leaned the broom against the central pillar, I do not think he expected it to stay there. This led us to think that Edward might be interested in the movement from <u>vertical</u> to <u>horizontal</u>.

We thought that Edward might be interested in the intermediate position between vertical and horizontal. Athey (1990, p. 134) described children's interest in 'the tree falling, the shot man falling and the person falling out of bed' as representing 'objects in intermediate positions between the horizontal and vertical'. Her explanation is that children are developing 'greater mobility of thought' through these sorts of explorations including 'falling down games'.

Another action that was of interest to us, was kicking the broom and rolled-up mat under a seat. This may have been something he had observed an adult do, but, again, it took real skill and strength to achieve. Again, the result was that both objects went from the <u>vertical</u> position to the <u>horizontal</u> position.

In terms of relationships, Winnicott (1975, p. 275) talked about 'The child's play at throwing things away … is an indication of the child's growing ability to master loss'. Winnicott was referring to the early play of infants but maybe these explorations continue. Shaw (1991, p. 64) offered another explanation, stating that 'Flinging away could express anger at mother for going away'. However, this explanation seemed less likely at this stage as we saw Edward grow in confidence and his deep involvement in play reflected this confidence.

Around the time that we observed Edward playing at cleaning, we also observed him engaging with other materials and children, in play connected to his exploration of <u>vertical</u> to <u>horizontal</u>, for example,

- Dragging the hoover and lying it down (3:9:16).

- Sitting on a plank on a step and leaning forward to move the plank into the <u>oblique</u> position (3:9:30).

- Manipulating the visor (3:9:30).

- Asking me to show him himself on camera, that involved me in turning the small screen towards Edward, from <u>vertical</u> to <u>horizontal</u> to <u>vertical</u> (180 degrees) (4:0:6).

- Manipulating a ladder outside with his friend and leaning it against various different structures (4:3:8).

However, one activity that took up a lot of Edward's time and effort was learning to ride a two-wheeler bike.

Observation: Edward and the falling over game

Edward (4:3:19), Julie and Kate each had a two-wheeler bike. A line of about 10 children were riding around the wall and down the ramp in front of the nursery. Edward stopped briefly when a bike had fallen over and Maureen (adult) was comforting Michael. He stopped but did not look towards Maureen and Michael.

The children circuited the wall several times. Then Kate and Julie got off their bikes and lay them down on the ground, then got back on. All three raced around the wall. Kate fell off. Edward was in front of her, stopped but did not look around, and then carried on. I said 'Edward'. Someone said 'Kate fell'. He rode all the way around to where Kate was lying on the ground under her bike. I suggested that he move the bike so that she could get up. He looked, gave a little smile and then moved the bike and then Kate got up. They continued their game.

After another circuit, Kate initiated a 'falling over' game. Kate 'fell' on her back on the ground. Julie pushed her bike over and sat on it. Edward pushed his bike over and walked around it looking at it lying on the ground. Then he sat on the ground, then on the bike, before picking it up and riding it onto the grass.

The two girls joined him and all three sat on the grass with their bikes lying on the ground near them. Kate said they were having a 'picnic'. Edward said they were having 'dinner'. Julie said 'I don't cry when I fall on the grass'. I said 'I think

(Continued)

(Continued)

you would if you hurt yourself'. Kate got up and demonstrated 'Watch me' and fell over. Then Edward got up, ran a short distance and then threw himself onto the grass, lying on his back with his arms outstretched above his head. As he ran he said, 'Watch me, I'm going to the ...?' He ran back to his friends and sat down with his legs crossed and his hand resting on his bike. Kate began singing about 'Getting stuck up the tree'. Edward stood up and walked around his bike, leaning it carefully against the fence in an almost vertical position. Julie got on her bike and rode away and then Edward followed.

DISCUSSION AND INTERPRETATION OF EDWARD'S ACTIONS AND COMMUNICATION

In schema terms, Edward seemed to be interested in how objects and people go from the vertical to the horizontal position and back to the vertical. He was interested in what his bike looked like, lying on the ground, as well as feeling what it was like in a vertical position, with him riding it.

Alongside his intellectual interest in the movement and configuration, were his feelings about what was going on when someone fell. In relationship terms, Edward seemed slightly anxious when Michael was being comforted. When his friend, Kate, fell off her bike, he stopped but did not look around. This may have been because he was anxious about his friend. It was interesting that Kate waited until Edward rode all the way back around to where she was, so that he could lift the bike out of the way for her to get up. Maybe this was a game they had played before? I wonder whether his little smile was a smile of pleasure, relief or even embarrassment?

The small group seemed to move from this genuine 'falling off' to symbolically representing 'falling over'. This was a way of 'playing with' the idea. Maybe they felt such 'masters of bike riding' that they rarely fell off and could begin to 'play with' falling off.

Edward did not fall over on the tarmac but did join in when they were on the grass. So the game developed into one of 'falling over and not getting hurt'. In terms of Edward's possible anxiety about other children getting hurt, this was a way to explore how it feels to fall over and survive, reasonably unscathed. The game may have provided a 'container' for his anxiety about 'falling over'.

SO WHAT?

Throughout this period of time, Edward seemed to go from the physical movement, strongly motivated by his overwhelming emotions, through exploring by using several objects, to the concept of 'falling over and not getting hurt'. There may have been no connection between Edward throwing himself on the floor in distress and his subsequent exploration of objects and people falling over. However, his discomfort or uncertainty when other children fell over indicated that he was unsure about how badly they were hurt. An enduring concern seemed to be with 'fixing' or reinstating objects or people to their former states.

Maybe, Edward's initial hypothesis was that anything broken was broken forever and his emerging hypothesis was that there are degrees of hurt and that broken objects can be fixed. He was only prepared to take very small risks in relation to people, for example falling over on soft ground, but could take much greater risks in his explorations with objects.

The other evidence presented here to support the idea that Edward was exploring, not only the intellectual concept of 'together and apart' with objects, but also the associated feelings about being separated from and reunited with his mother, in particular, is only one perspective on his actions. It is certainly a perspective that would be recognised in the field of psychotherapy or play therapy (Winnicott, 2006). The question I have had to constantly ask myself is whether this kind of perspective and understanding is helpful to workers and to children and families using mainstream services.

Susan Isaacs was a teacher and a psychoanalyst, and was keen to differentiate between the two roles. She acknowledged that her psychoanalytic training had given her insights into the children's inner worlds but she insisted that 'play' was the key to meeting the needs of young children, both intellectually and emotionally (1933, p. 428). The emphasis in the Malting House School was on freedom of expression and the acceptance of and interest in the whole range of behaviours displayed by the children. This work affirms the importance of play to young children.

When I was using a purely cognitive focus to analyse children's schemas, I seemed to be missing out on a great deal of the information available. I was not accepting or deeply interested in all of the children's motives and behaviours. However, having become aware of these possible links between cognition and emotion, I am aware that I notice when there is an action that might relate to the emotional life of the child. This is happening increasingly frequently. I am more open to children's and adults' expressions of emotion and identifying schemas is one way of tuning in to children's motives for action.

Table 5.1 Schemas mentioned and links made

Connecting and disconnecting	Edward seemed to gain satisfaction from seeing objects connected, i.e. hook to eye
Vertical (position)	Edward took an interest in learning to ride a two-wheeler bike and in placing objects in an upright position leaning against walls, trees, etc.
Horizontal (position)	Edward was also interested in what happened when objects fell or were placed or kicked in a horizontal position
Going through a boundary	Edward used a 'going through a boundary' action to connect the hook to the eye
Proximity and separation	Edward seemed to be interested in objects being together and apart, possibly connected to an interest in proximity and separation
Enclosing	Edward tried enclosing to fix or connect
Enveloping	Edward enveloped a larger area of the floor by making sure that two mats were perfectly overlapped
Containing	Edward deliberately placed the rolled up mats in the corner of the cloakroom, a perfect space to hold them in place
Oblique (position)	Edward placed objects in an oblique position and also gave attention to keeping the mop and brush in that position while using them
Trajectory	Edward threw and kicked the mats and brush under a seat

SUGGESTED FURTHER READING

Athey, C. (1990) *Extending Thought in Young Children*, Paul Chapman, London.

Athey, C. (2007) *Extending Thought in Young Children*, 2nd edn, Paul Chapman, London.

Bowlby, J. (1997) *Attachment and Loss Volume 1*, Pimlico, London.

Bowlby, J. (1998) *Attachment and Loss Volume 2*, Pimlico, London.

Winnicott, D.W. (2006) *The Family and Individual Development*, Routledge Classics, London.

Sam: Enveloping, Containing and Seriating to Understand Separation and Loss and the Distribution of Power

---

In this chapter we introduce:

- Sam and her family

- Observations of Sam and her friend, Diane, <u>enveloping</u> objects

- Observations of Sam exploring ideas about power and strength

---

INTRODUCTION AND CONTEXT

Sam was 3 years 10 months and 15 days when I first observed her for this study. She was already in her second year at nursery and was attending four mornings and staying for lunch.

Sam has two older sisters, who were aged 5 and 18 at the beginning of the study. They lived with their mum and dad locally. Sam was the only child I studied whose family I did not already know quite well at the start of the study.

Sam had what Katey (Deputy Head of Centre) described as a sort of 'other world' quality about her. She was quite serious and intense, and was often observed acting out stories.

At the beginning of this study, she had developed a close relationship with Diane, who shared her interests (Arnold, 1990). Towards the end of that year, she was playing with other children, mostly boys. Sam expressed her wish to be a boy and nearly always took on the male role in her stories and role play games.

Observations and discussions made over one year were used to inform our thinking about Sam and her expressions and representations of emotion and attachment. Within this case study I have drawn on samples of the observations to illustrate two themes that emerged from the data on Sam:

- An interest in <u>enveloping</u> and <u>containing</u> to represent sleep, jail and death.

- An interest in exploring <u>seriation</u> to understand power and vulnerability.

CONTEXT OF THE OBSERVATIONS

I noticed Sam's 'other world' quality right away. She was often deeply involved in play with her friend, Diane. On some days she seemed faintly amused and quite pleased that I was following her. On other days, she avoided me by moving away and, on one occasion, she got inside a small play tent and closed the zip. Whenever I felt that she was uncomfortable with my interest in her play, I stopped filming and moved away.

Sam was fairly articulate when I began studying her, so she was often revealing her inner world through her actions *and* language. She was close to her Family Worker, Margaret, and also to Katey (Deputy Head of Centre) with whom she sat at lunchtime.

Sam spent long periods of time exploring with animal figures. She also enjoyed using the train set and puppets. In this first observation, Sam and Diane developed a storyline while playing at the child height sinks in the bathroom.

<u>ENVELOPING</u> AND <u>CONTAINING</u>

Observation: Sam and Diane playing at the sink

Sam (3:10:15) and Diane each stood in front of an individual sink in the children's bathroom area. They had plugged each sink with a paper towel and were turning the water on and off. They went into the main nursery room to get some animal figures. Sam came back carrying a 'billie goat' which she manipulated in different ways. She placed it in different positions both in and out of the water, claiming it was 'bigger' than Diane's figure and that she was making a 'bigger shower' as her sink was 'really full up'. Sam held her figure under the water and exclaimed 'Mine's bigger – mine's bigger'. Diane agreed 'Really big – I can't get in there'. Sam suggested getting 'the other animals'. She was using an American accent.

DISCUSSION AND INTERPRETATION OF SAM AND DIANE'S ACTIONS AND COMMUNICATION

Using schema theory to understand the play, the two girls had co-ordinated several schemas here. Each had stuffed the plughole with a paper towel to create a <u>container</u> for water and to stop the water from <u>going through the boundary</u> of the pipe under the sink. They were using a <u>horizontal trajectory movement</u> to make the water go on and off. Sam seemed interested in <u>positioning</u> her billie goat in different places suggesting an interest in space. Athey (1990, p. 110) suggested that children explore topological space by positioning objects and gradually make the shift to understanding projective space when 'objects or figures are represented from different points of view'. Sam introduced comparative size, as a concept, showing an interest in <u>seriation</u>. While holding her billie goat under the water or <u>enveloping</u> it with water, she noticed the effect, magnification.

Using attachment theory to understand the play, the friends were being connected, to some extent, through mirroring each other's actions, but also expressing their wish to have the 'bigger one'. This may have been about wishing to feel more powerful. If Sam's sink was 'really full up' then she had managed to do this more quickly than Diane. So she was 'doing' most and 'having' most, which may have resulted in her feeling more powerful. Diane offered some rationalisation when she said 'I'm making a little shower' inferring that bigger was not necessarily better. Diane did acknowledge the effect of holding the billie goat under water and that there appeared to be no room for her or her animal figure.

This was the first time I observed Sam and I was mindful of not intruding into the play of an established dyad. They seemed to be providing a 'secure base' for each other at nursery from which they could explore issues. Berlin and Cassidy (1999, p. 692) pointed out that 'secure infant–mother attachments go hand in hand with more harmonious sibling interactions and friendship quality and quantity'. So Sam's ability to have a close friend to confide in may be linked with her early relationship with her mother. According to Berlin and Cassidy, surprisingly, there is currently no evidence of infant–father attachments impacting in the same way.

Observation: Sam and Diane develop their storyline at the sink

The play continued when they came back carrying some more figures.

Sam	*'Hey baby'.*
Diane	*'What is it daddy?'*
Sam	*'Look at this big crocodile'.*
Diane	*'Ask him what his name is'.*
Sam	*'Pretend daddy died and she cried for him'.*
Diane	*'Poor daddy' (makes crying noise).*
Diane	*'Pretend daddy died in the water'.*
Sam	*'Died in the big water'.*

They continued manipulating the figures and placing them in different positions around the sink and towel dispenser.

Diane suggested 'Pretend they're dying in the big water'.

Sam placed a dinosaur onto the towel container then into the water.

Sam said 'He's going alive' as she jumped the dinosaur over to Diane's sink, removed the paper towel plugs from both sinks making the water disappear.

DISCUSSION AND INTERPRETATION OF SAM AND DIANE'S ACTIONS AND COMMUNICATION

Using schema theory, Sam seemed to link <u>enveloping</u> with water with dying (or maybe drowning, although neither child mentioned drowning). Sam made the point that it was in 'the big water'.

Again Sam placed an animal figure in different positions and linked movement with 'going alive'. <u>Transformation</u> is an aspect of schematic exploration that seems to be prevalent at this age (Arnold, 1997, p. 281). Young children are naturally interested in their effect on objects and on people. Sam may have been hypothesising about how people die and how and whether they 'go alive' again. She was using movement to represent symbolically that in their game, the daddy was 'going alive'. Athey (1990, p. 201) pointed out that sometimes 'transformations' are 'anticipated in the mind with some difficulty'. How can any of us understand the transformation from alive to dead without first-hand experiences? Corsaro (2003, p. 103) described how some children he observed played out 'death–rebirth themes' in their fantasy play. He pointed out that the children 'are frequently exposed to information about illness, dying and death by the media' but that they also use information from 'fairy tales and Disney movies' in their play.

Using attachment theory Sam may have been exploring ideas about separation and loss in relation to her daddy or to people in general. Corsaro (2003, p. 107) said that the 'production of death–rebirth themes in spontaneous fantasy enables them to share concerns or fears they have about death'. Sam's mum worked in an old people's home at this time, so death was a common topic of conversation at home.

Again, I felt that I was possibly intruding into the world of an established dyad. Sam and Diane seemed barely aware of my presence. Maybe my discomfort was connected to my own fears about separation, loss and death.

The two girls moved from this play into the construction area and spent a short time *'making an <u>enclosure</u> with fencing and placing some animals inside, saying that the farmyard was "shut"'*.

Later that morning they developed the idea of dinosaurs as 'baddies'.

Observation: Sam and Diane develop their ideas about dinosaurs as baddies

Sam and Diane were at either side of the water tray in the main nursery room.

Diane	*'Mama, mama – something near me'.*
Sam	*'Hey watch this – I think it's a dragon'.*
	(She held up a Tyrranosaurus Rex)
Sam	*'I want this one – I will get this one' (deep voice).*
Diane	*'Darling'.*
Sam	*'What?'*
Diane	*'Are you crying like a nitty?'*

Sam had a dinosaur in each hand and leant across and put them into the water, saying 'I'm never coming near them'.

(Continued)

(Continued)

Sam	*'Pretend he doesn't wake up'.*
	'Where did you come from?' She was holding an elephant and a billie goat.
	'I kill dinosaurs'.
	'I kill these ones'.
	'Watch me' ...

Both girls moved to the middle area of the room carrying their figures.

Sam	*'Tend that was a baddie as well – his brother' (pointing at the dinosaur she was holding).*
	'It smells like ... poo'.
	'Lets fight em again'. She held the dinosaur as though it was eating the billie goat.
	'Let's fight him'. There were three billie goats on the floor.

Sam and Diane were each holding a dinosaur who pounced on the billie goats as though eating them (Sam licked her lips).

DISCUSSION AND INTERPRETATION OF SAM AND DIANE'S ACTIONS AND COMMUNICATION

Using schema theory, again Sam immersed or <u>enveloped</u> the dinosaurs in water and then suggested 'Pretend he doesn't wake up'. She seemed to be representing a sleeping dinosaur.

The dinosaurs were <u>classified</u> or grouped as 'baddies' who even 'smelt like poo'. Sam and Diane used the dinosaur figures to kill the smaller and weaker animals, possibly <u>classified</u> as goodies. Killing them involved eating them. So the weaker or smaller animal would be eaten by and <u>contained</u> inside the stronger or bigger animals.

Using attachment theory, Sam represented the temporary absence created by sleeping. When she said 'Pretend he doesn't wake up', she may have meant at that moment or permanently. She may still have been exploring her concerns about death.

Also a bad smell was projected onto the dinosaurs. So they were 'baddies' but they were also strong and could 'engulf' weaker creatures. Some of Sam's play seemed to involve 'as if I were stronger' behaviour.

Even before I began to study Sam, her Family Worker, Margaret, had commented on Sam often using wild animal figures, for example, lions and tigers. We were curious about whether having a wild ferocious animal in her hand, made her feel stronger and more powerful. It certainly seemed to help her to express ideas about being strong but also to express her fear that strong animals (or people) eat up weaker ones.

Later on that morning the two girls played with animal figures in the Beach Area.

Observation: Sam and Diane bury animal figures in the sand

Towards the end of the morning, both girls are in the Beach Area playing with figures again.

Sam (*in a deep voice*)	*'When I go to bed I get sick – really sick'. She buried the T-rex by putting handfuls of sand on top and patting and squeezing the sand around the T-rex.*
Sam	*'This panda bear's going in his bed – he's a good boy'. She buried the panda.*
	Sam took the dinosaur out and said in a deep voice:
	'It's time to go to sleep'.
	'I wanted to talk to you'.
	'Now go to sleep'.
	'And don't wake me up for no minutes – I'll tell you'. She buried the T-rex.
Sam	*'Rainbow – it's time to get up'.*

She lifted the T-rex out of the sand and crawled, walking two figures/animals to the edge of the sand.

She walked them back saying 'We're nearly there'.

She stopped in the middle of the Beach Area and buried the panda.

Sam	*'I be sick and I tired'.*
Diane	*'I be sick'.*

DISCUSSION AND INTERPRETATION OF SAM AND DIANE'S ACTIONS AND COMMUNICATION

Using schema theory to understand, Sam was using the sand to <u>envelop</u> the figures. She was using these actions as a symbolic representation of 'going to bed', 'getting sick' and 'going to sleep'. She also reversed her actions by uncovering the figures to represent waking up.

Using attachment theory, Sam was experimenting with making the figures disappear by <u>enveloping</u> them with sand. Her conversation with T-rex about not 'waking me up for no minutes' sounded very like a parent/child conversation at bedtime. We have seen in other case studies that this fear of separation and wish to stay near sometimes manifests itself at bedtime (Arnold, 2007).

I have become aware of the close connections, conceptually, between sleep, sickness and death. Any idea of death as a permanent separation brings with it the fear of not waking up from sleep and how to cope with it if it happens to a loved one.

Towards the end of the morning, both girls painted at the easel. Sam ended up '<u>*enveloping*</u> *her hands back and front with black paint, before going to the bathroom to wash it off*'.

In the next observation, made five weeks later, both girls revisited the idea of dying, this time using a large tray of lentils to cover their animals.

Observation: Sam and Diane explore ideas while playing with animal figures and lentils

Sam (3:11:22) and Diane were at opposite sides of a large water tray containing lentils. Sam was holding a polar bear figure and Diane was holding a panda figure.

They seemed to set the scene at first:

Sam	*'That's the Mummy bear and that's the Daddy bear'.*
Diane	*'And it was raining'.*
Sam	*'And they goed under there so they didn't get wet' (putting animals under shade).*
Diane	*'Pretend that was Daddy rain and Mummy rain'.*
Sam	*'Pretend that was their food and the food was ready – yummy'.*

They picked up lentils and let them drop onto the tray (like rain).

Diane	'Pretend it was raining'.
Sam	'I'm going to eat my dinner'. (She moved the bear to the bowl of lentils, making loud eating noises and dispersing the lentils with the bear.)

They seemed to develop a storyline about the Mummy and Daddy:

Diane	'Pretend Dad died ... pretend Dad died and Mummy didn't die'.
Sam	'Pretend Mummy was having a bath' (covering her bear with lentils).
Sam	'Pretend Dad was sleeping in his nice warm bed'. 'Pretend he was sleeping and Mummy got out of her bed and she waked Dad up'.
Diane	'Why?'
Sam	'Cos she did. She's beautiful – you have to do it'.

Then they enacted their storyline:

Diane	'Wake up! Wake up!'
Sam	(in a deep voice) 'What do you want to say?'
Diane	[Can't hear response] ... 'Why is it night time?'

Then Sam took the storyline in a different direction:

Sam	'Pretend Daddy's gone. Pretend Daddy's gone to jail' (as she placed her bear inside a hollow block which was on the floor near her).

DISCUSSION AND INTERPRETATION OF SAM AND DIANE'S ACTIONS AND COMMUNICATION

Using schema theory, Sam immediately established that she was holding and acting on behalf of the 'daddy figure' and that Diane was representing the 'mummy figure'. There was little difference in size in this instance, although 'daddy' and 'mummy' may have inferred some sort of <u>seriation</u> in relation to size, power or strength. Diane's use of the lentils to create 'daddy rain' and 'mummy rain' also inferred strength or size.

Sam was able to articulate the function of a plank, which was across the top of the tray. The figures staying dry were functionally dependent on being covered or <u>enveloped</u> by the plank (like a sort of roof).

Diane introduced the idea of death. As Sam scooped lentils with her hand and poured them onto the 'daddy figure', she talked about 'Mummy having a bath'. As Diane was also pouring lentils onto the 'mummy figure', it seems reasonable to deduce that the two girls were symbolically representing having a bath by covering or <u>enveloping</u> their figures with lentils.

Sam went on to talk about 'Dad sleeping in his nice, warm bed', again represented by <u>enveloping</u> the figure with lentils. Diane talked about 'night time' when darkness <u>envelops</u> the light.

Finally Sam removed her figure from the tray and placed it inside a hollow block so that it was hidden from sight (or <u>contained</u>). This time she talked about pretending that 'Daddy has gone to jail', symbolically represented by being inside the block.

Using attachment theory to understand Sam's actions, she immediately established that she was exploring how it felt to be the 'Daddy'. The plank may have represented protection from the 'rain' and also a 'secure base' from which to explore.

Sam played with ideas about separation. When 'Mummy was taking a bath', this may have involved a brief separation. Similarly, sleep, even together in the same bed, involves separation for a while. Finally, Sam experimented with a longer separation by representing 'Daddy gone to jail'. Although Diane talked about 'Daddy dying', Sam did not verbalise this on this occasion.

Both Jane (Sam's mother) and Margaret (her Family Worker) commented on the fact that Sam wanted to be a boy. Jane said that Sam would take on the male role, as she saw males as bigger and stronger. She also liked animals and vampires, and tended to choose the scarier roles to play.

However, she also wanted to keep the whole family together. Sam told her mum 'I'm going to marry all of you – you, daddy, Lucy, Mia and Mousie – but Mousie's dead'. Jane thought that by 'marrying' Sam meant 'connected' or 'together'. Sam may have been thinking about how she could be reunited with her pet mouse, who was dead.

I am convinced that most of these explorations were connected to understanding separation and loss, how it feels and when it is reversible. Sam listened to and created lots of stories at this time. She enjoyed videos and would often re-enact what she had heard or seen in her play.

Winnicott's idea of 'play' involved the creative space between parent and child, 'the transitional space' (1991, p. 68). Sam seemed to be using this space and time to explore her fears about what might happen and how it would feel. Her main concern seemed to be with the 'daddy figure'. She could be one removed from him by using a figure to represent him, rather than by playing the role of the daddy herself.

Later on that morning, she spoke about *'losing a load of fireworks'*. It was the day after Bonfire Night and Sam spoke about having *'left them in a taxi'*. This small loss may have been experienced by the family the night before and, again, put Sam in touch with the feeling of loss.

About a month after this observation, I met Jane. We had arranged a meeting that she could not attend. She told me, *'Sam is completely preoccupied with death'*. There had been no recent deaths in the family to spark this interest, although Jane often mentioned one of the old people she worked with dying, for example, *'Midge died today'*. Recently Sam was talking about death and then said *'I want to see my dad'*. Jane said *'He'll be home soon'*. Sam said *'I want to see my dad **now**'*.

EXPLORING SERIATION TO UNDERSTAND POWER AND VULNERABILITY

From a very young age, children begin recognising and classifying objects in their world according to similarities and differences. Much research evidence has built on the reactions of even very young babies to seeing something new (Gopnik et al., 1999). Most young children explore ideas about seriation and these ideas become increasingly refined at around the age of 3–4. 'Seriation' was defined by Piaget and Inhelder (1969, p. 101) as 'arranging elements according to increasing or decreasing size'. The form, as well as size, includes other features.

An early differentiation, typically voiced by young children, is 'mummy, daddy and baby'. These differences in size and other features have been exemplified in traditional stories such as 'Goldilocks and The Three Bears'. What usually follows is the co-ordination of different features and some anomalies, for example, the Gentle Giant.

When these observations were made, Sam was very interested in using pretend play to explore the comparative strength and power of this triad of mummy, daddy and baby. As other children have, she also used the terms 'mummy, daddy and baby' to symbolise strength, size or power (Arnold, 1999, p. 68).

Within the environment of the nursery, there were some fairly boisterous children. Sam did not like loud noises and could be intimidated by noisy children. She could, however, seek the help of adults when necessary. So Sam's exploration of power, fears and friction may have related both to her personal experiences in the nursery at that time as well as to her inner fears about power and strength. All of the observations presented up to now in this chapter contain aspects relating to power, strength and size. Sam seemed to use whatever was at hand to continue to explore some of the same issues.

Observation: At the trains

Sam (3:11:7) and Diane went to the middle area and knelt down at the train-set. Sam looked around and seemed to be singing to herself.

Sam seemed to set the scene for the play:

She placed three carriages in a line on the track, then said 'Gonna get this big one'. She moved away and picked up a large, blue engine. She placed it at the front of the engines and knocked other carriages in front off the track with her other hand, saying 'Not, not, not, not!'

She ran her train along the track and into the shed, saying 'Daddy was sleeping'.

They seemed to begin the story:

Sam   *'Momma, momma'.*

She looked around, got another train and repeated 'Momma, momma' and 'I don't know where my daddy is'.

Diane   *'Dadda ... daddy'.*

Sam ran her train back along the track.

Diane   *'Daddy, don't go away'.*

Sam   *'Mummy watch ... daddy back to his bed' as she ran the train back into the shed. [Sam was talking quietly throughout. I only caught bits of what she said.] Diane ran a red engine into the shed and said 'Me too'.*

> *Sam seemed to suggest a development of the story:*
>
> *Each of them took an engine from the shed.*
>
> **Sam**   *'Let's go this way' as she ran an engine down a fork in the track towards two tunnels saying 'Chooo'. Reversed and repeated this. Her engine ran through the two tunnels and she retrieved it from the end of the second tunnel. Sam then ran her engine into the shed.*

DISCUSSION AND INTERPRETATION OF SAM AND DIANE'S ACTIONS AND COMMUNICATION·

Using schema theory to understand the play, Sam was co-ordinating several schemas: <u>connecting</u> carriages to make a <u>line</u>; attributing the role of 'daddy' to the biggest engine (<u>seriation</u>); running her train in a <u>trajectory</u> until it was <u>contained</u> inside the shed; and, running her train so that it <u>went through the boundary</u> of the two tunnels.

Using attachment theory to understand the play, Sam was once again exploring the idea of 'daddy sleeping', a brief separation, symbolised by putting the engine into the shed. She also introduced with her voice, a baby or child searching for her daddy. Diane took on the role of the mummy imploring the daddy not to go away. Sam also used the two tunnels and may have been representing 'going through' 'darkness' or 'a dark time'(?) before coming out of the other side and returning to the safety of the shed.

This was filmed in the middle of the busy nursery without any special sound equipment. So, although I could not hear everything that was said, I believe I picked up the essence of the play. The intonation used by the two children conveyed some of the feelings they were portraying.

Observation: A boy takes the mummy train

This observation shows what happened when a boy took a train they were using:

A boy came over, saying 'That was my train' and took the red engine.

Sam turned around to me and said 'He nicked that off Diane'.

Me   *'He seems to think it was his before it was yours'.*

Sam   *'That's the mummy one'.*

Me   *'You could go and ask him for it back ... or you could have another one to be the mummy ... what do you think?'*

Sam   *'We need a big, long one'.*

Me   *'You need a big, long one to be the mummy? No other big, long ones ... look in there ... see if there's any? ... Maybe it could be a little mummy this time?'*

Sam   *'Got this one' (holding one up).*

Me   *'That's a nice one isn't it? So that one's going to be the mummy is it?'*

Sam threw a stripey engine towards Diane and said 'That's the mummy'.

Both children continued running their engines along the track, through the two tunnels.

DISCUSSION AND INTERPRETATION OF SAM AND DIANE'S ACTIONS AND COMMUNICATION

Using schema theory to understand, the main emphasis here was on the comparative size of a 'mummy' train, which needed to be 'big and long' (seriation). Having sorted the trains into sizes, Sam was not easily satisfied that another train could represent the 'mummy'. Finally, she compromised by selecting 'a stripey engine' to represent the mummy. Both children continued to run their trains in a trajectory, through the boundary of the two tunnels.

Using attachment theory to understand, Sam looked slightly threatened by the boy taking the 'mummy' train away. The mummy going away was not part of their storyline. Sam knew I was nearby and immediately turned to me. She may have expected me to intervene to protect the play. I offered ideas about what to do. Neither Sam nor Diane was prepared to confront the boy so the only alternative was to select another train to be the mummy. Sam and Diane's goal seemed to be to continue and maintain the game.

I became aware, when viewing this clip repeatedly, that I talked a lot during this sequence. I think I was genuinely responding to Sam. I hoped that Sam and Diane would feel strong enough to protest and ask for the train back. Sam's tone suggested that this was a moral issue and that the boy had behaved unfairly. She may have seen the boy as an aggressor whom she was not willing or able to confront. What may have been presented to the children, in real life, was a power issue linked to gender.

I could have intervened on their behalf but would I have taken away the power of the two girls to deal with this in their own way? I tried to offer some options and waited to see what happened.

Sam and Diane continued to play with ideas about power and strength by:

- Being dogs in the home corner, who were bossed around by other children (3:11:29).

- Being chased by boys outside, feeling threatened but also knowing they could ask adults for help and with the added advantage of being 'four' years old (4:04:19).

Sam subsequently seemed to move away from playing with Diane as often, and was observed with adults:

- In conversation with Margaret about *'going on a ghost train'* and not feeling too scared as her dad was with her (4:04:19).

- Being a *'white lion'* with Katey at lunchtime, moving very slowly and roaring. Katey introduced the idea that this *'powerful animal might be lonely and sad'* (a paradox?) (4:05:06).

When re-enacting a story with Margaret, Margaret skilfully offered Sam an option to be strong and powerful.

Observation: Re-enacting a story with Margaret

(Playing a game in which the daddy giraffe has been injured and has 'black stuff' on him, that is, blood)

Margaret and Sam seemed to set the scene:

Sam (4:04:19) was holding a large and a medium giraffe.

Margaret said 'Earthquake'.

Sam picked up the medium giraffe, put it on the table and shrieked 'Earthquake coming, earthquake coming'. Margaret moved the cloth to simulate the earth shaking.

Margaret   'Earth shake'.

The story began:

Sam   'Mummy needs to take care of her little one'.

Margaret took the medium and little giraffes. 'Stay close darling – we can't help daddy now'. 'I'll look after you – you stay close to me'.

Sam stood the daddy up.

Sam   'Daddy's …'

Margaret   'Are daddies powerful? Are daddies strong?'

Sam stood the large giraffe near a tree. 'Daddy can reach …'.

Margaret   'Daddy, daddy I can't reach'. Sam put the little giraffe on the daddy's neck near the top of the tree.

Another child posed a threat:

Stephen banged an animal on the table. Sam covered one ear and said, 'That hurt my ears'. Margaret pointed to a picture of a giraffe on the wall and said, 'Do you remember what it did? Do you remember what noise it made?' Sam moved her mouth. Margaret made a sound.

Another threat:

Sam picked up a dinosaur.

> **Margaret**   'Oh something dangerous is coming to the Great Valley'. Sam placed the dinosaur on the table and opened and closed her mouth as she manipulated the dinosaur's mouth.
>
> **Margaret** whispered to Stephen 'Something scary's coming into the Great Valley'.
>
> *Daniel approached (in a skeleton outfit).*
>
> **Sam** said, 'Skeleton!' Stephen held up two fierce animals and banged them on the table. Sam continued to manipulate the dinosaur's mouth and to make a roaring sound. Margaret encouraged Stephen to run away and hide and went with him.
>
> **Margaret** announced 'Samisaurus!'
>
> *Sam moved towards Stephen and Margaret holding the dinosaur figure. Stephen roared.*

DISCUSSION AND INTERPRETATION OF SAM'S ACTIONS AND COMMUNICATION

Using schema theory to understand the play, Sam was using the three giraffes to represent daddy, mummy and baby and also their relative sizes and strength (<u>seriation</u>). Margaret moved the cloth in a side-to-side <u>trajectory</u> to represent the earth shaking. Sam used <u>seriation</u> again, to think about the mummy caring for her little one in the sense that the mother was bigger and stronger and could protect the baby. She also made reference to the daddy's height. He was the tallest and could reach higher than the mummy or baby (<u>seriation</u>). Stephen introduced a very loud sound (louder in terms of <u>seriation</u> than Sam could tolerate). Margaret reminded Sam of the noise made by a real giraffe they had seen together at the zoo. Sam introduced a dinosaur. The dinosaur represented something fierce and dangerous, a more powerful creature than the giraffe (<u>seriation</u>). Although Stephen once again made a loud noise, Sam continued to play the part of the dangerous dinosaur, more powerful than Stephen (<u>seriation</u>). Margaret's suggestion of 'Samisaurus' offered Sam the chance to see herself as more powerful than the noisy and boisterous boys in nursery.

Using attachment theory to understand, the simulated earthquake offered a context in which weaker creatures were under threat. Sam talked about the 'mummy taking care of her little one' which Bowlby saw as the purpose of attachment. Margaret introduced the idea of 'staying close' and not being able to 'help daddy now', suggesting that the mummy and baby could be saved but not the daddy. When Sam suggested that the 'daddy could reach', Margaret immediately offered a way that the daddy could help the baby to reach the top of the tree.

When Stephen's banging seemed to threaten Sam, Margaret did not reassure her but reminded her of the noise made by real giraffes at the zoo. It was as if to say, you have been brave and have experienced the noise of a real giraffe and this is only a child banging a toy on the table.

One of Sam's favourite stories was 'The Lion, the Witch and the Wardrobe', so Margaret's reference to the Great Valley tuned in to that interest. Somehow Margaret helped Sam to become the powerful one, the chaser, by referring to her figure as 'Samisaurus'.

Sam seemed to be playing with ideas about power, strength and survival, particularly in relation to the daddy. He was bigger and stronger than the mummy and baby, although in this storyline, he was injured and may not have survived. There was a sort of paradox here for Sam. He was the strongest and yet he was injured and this made him weak. Margaret very skilfully enabled Sam to represent a strong role and to be an aggressor in the real life of the nursery.

BRINGING THE OBSERVATIONS TOGETHER

Throughout the year that Sam was studied at nursery, she seemed to be exploring ideas about temporary and permanent absence and also issues to do with power and strength.

Sadly, Sam's parents separated towards the end of the year during which she was studied. In retrospect, it seemed no coincidence that she spent a great deal of time exploring separation and loss through her play at this time. She seemed particularly concerned with the daddy and what life would be like for him and for the family without him. Perhaps Sam was motivated to <u>envelop</u> objects in order to understand about presence and absence and to gain some control of her feelings of loss.

Her anxiety about her dad's strength and survival seemed to be played out through her interest in families of animals and trains, using <u>seriation</u> to think about and feel the power of the different objects. Towards the end of the year, a paradox seemed to emerge. Sam may have been wondering whether biggest is always most powerful or strongest.

SO WHAT?

What seems most valuable and applicable to other children in settings are:

- The long periods of uninterrupted play, 'free flow play' as described by Bruce (2004, p. 149) that Sam was able to engage in alongside partners of her choice, both adults and children.

- The adult knowledge and support for Sam with her explorations, both from her parents and workers and the willingness of adults to enter Sam's world and be her 'companions' (Trevarthen, 2002).

- The trust built up over time between Sam's family and the nursery workers.

- The resources that were available for Sam to try out <u>containing</u> and <u>enveloping</u> in different ways, that resulted in different effects. Sam had access to sand, water and paint at all times, both indoors and out. As part of the workshop environment, she could use various construction and small world resources at any time. In addition, she could use dough, clay, lentils and wet spaghetti some of the time. Several 'families' of animals were purchased for the nursery, with Sam in mind.

Table 6.1 Schemas mentioned and links made

Enveloping	Sam seemed to envelop different objects with different materials to symbolise concepts like 'sleep', 'death' and 'jail'
Containing	Sometimes Sam contained objects inside other objects similarly symbolising 'here and gone' in different ways
Seriating	Sam seemed very interested in sorting everything she played with into most powerful through to least powerful. Through this sorting she discovered some anomalies
Going through a boundary	Sam used tunnels and trains to practise 'going through a boundary'. This pattern may have signified 'going through' a difficult or dark time
Horizontal trajectory	Sam used this movement to turn the taps on and off and to run the trains along a line
Positioning	In the bathroom and elsewhere, Sam positioned animal figures and seemed to convey power differentials through this positioning
Transformation (not a repeated pattern as such but an aspect we notice children exploring)	Sam seemed interested in the transformation from alive to dead and the possibility of dead to 'going alive'

(Continued)

Table 6.1 *(Continued)*

Enclosing	Sam and Diane enclosed the animals and said the farmyard was 'shut'
Classifying or grouping according to certain shared features	Sam was interested in using families of animals, classifying them according to similarities. She also seemed to 'project' certain features on to certain animals, e.g. dinosaurs smelt like poo
Connecting	Sam connected the carriages together
Lines	Sam made lines with trains
Trajectory	Sam only seemed interested in the 'journey'. She ran trains along lines and into the shed to support her symbolic play. She did not seem interested in a circle of track to run trains around

SUGGESTED FURTHER READING

Anthony, S. (1940) *The Child's Discovery of Death*, Routledge, London.

Athey, C. (1990) *Extending Thought in Young Children*, Paul Chapman, London.

Athey, C. (2007) *Extending Thought in Young Children*, 2nd edn, Paul Chapman, London.

Arnold, C. (2003) *Observing Harry: Child Development and Learning 0–5years*, Open University Press, Maidenhead.

Corsaro, W.A. (2003) *We're Friends Right? Inside Kids' Culture*, Joseph Henry Press, Washington, DC.

Winnicott, D.W. (1991) *Playing and Reality*, Brunner-Routledge, Hove.

7

Susan: Containing, Enveloping and Going Through Boundaries

This chapter introduces:

- Susan and her family

- Observations of Susan shortly after starting nursery

- Changes that affect Susan

- Observations of Susan showing her ambivalent feelings towards her mother

INTRODUCTION AND CONTEXT

Susan was 2 years 11 months and 18 days when I first observed her for this study. She had recently started nursery and was attending four mornings each week. Susan lived with her mum and brother, Daniel, aged 9. A family friend, Joe, lodged at the house at that time. Susan saw her maternal grandmother ('bestest friend'), Aunt ('special friend') and Uncle ('little friend') every day. Her father, Mark, had left before Susan was born and, although he was referred to, she did not remember him. At nursery, Susan was very reserved and rarely revealed or expressed her feelings at this time.

I had known her mother, Sian, since she was a teenager, attending the youth club in our building. I was also involved with the family during the two years Daniel attended the nursery. Sian had attended one of the study groups I co-led and we had produced a portfolio about Daniel's special interests.

At first Susan was not well settled at nursery. She was a little unsure and often needed to be near an adult. Her Family Worker, chosen by Sian, was Danielle, because she was 'about my age and also knows about our family'.

Trevarthen (2003) says that 'emotions are the quality of movement'. Susan moved slowly. She spoke so quietly that it was difficult for others to hear her. She rarely allowed herself to express her feelings at nursery. It seemed that most of what I wanted to discover was hidden or unexpressed. In this case study issues about 'attachment' came to the fore and I found myself using 'attachment' theory before 'schema' theory in the discussion and interpretation of the observations of Susan.

Within the case study, I have focused on three sets of observations:

- tracking Susan for the first time

- changes

- Susan showing ambivalent feelings.

One main theme emerged from the data on Susan:

- An interest in <u>enveloping,</u> <u>containing</u> and <u>going through a boundary,</u> and how those actions might relate to Susan's understanding of relationships with others.

CONTEXT OF OBSERVATIONS

Although I did not know Susan prior to the study, she was aware of my connection to her family. She showed a level of trust in me and in other adults at the nursery that must have been rooted in her family's long-term relationship with people in the nursery and centre. Although Susan came to the nursery reluctantly at first, she showed signs of trusting adults at nursery, for example, if she got her top wet she would ask a Family Worker to help her get changed. She usually looked pleased to see me. She would give a little smile and seemed happy for me to observe her.

Although Susan was not like 'a fish in water' (Laevers, 1997), when I first observed her, she was able to explore the nursery environment a little and to have moments of deep 'involvement' (Laevers, 1997). The first three observations were made on the morning I tracked Susan for the first time.

TRACKING SUSAN FOR THE FIRST TIME

Observation: Susan arriving at nursery

Susan (2:11:18) was brought into nursery by Joe. She held onto his leg. He bent down and talked quietly to her. Annette picked Susan up so that Joe could leave, and carried her to the snack area and then put her down ... Susan walked around holding Annette's hand, while Annette prepared to set up a mirror and face painting ... Susan picked up a brush and put it into the water and then into the face paint and back into the water. She watched Annette painting other children's faces. Susan put red paint on a brush and then painted her own lips.

DISCUSSION AND INTERPRETATION OF SUSAN'S ACTIONS

Using attachment theory to understand, Susan held on to Joe's leg in an attempt to stay connected. He spoke quietly to her, so quietly that what he said was unheard by the workers. Annette became involved because she was nearest and because Danielle had been off work and Susan had settled with Annette more than once. So, although Danielle was at the nursery that day, Joe settled Susan with Annette, who was in the area nearest to the entrance. Sian told me that Susan was attracted to Annette 'because she wears make-up and nail varnish'. Neither Sian nor any of her friends wore make-up so this was a novelty for Susan.

Annette carried Susan at first, thereby 'holding' and 'containing' her feelings about being separated (Bion, 1962). It seemed significant that once Annette took Susan from Joe, Susan held onto her hand and went with her, wherever she went, suggesting that her goal was to stay near Annette, who she had felt safe with and had protected her at the nursery in the absence of Danielle (Cassidy, 1999, p. 7).

Using schema theory to understand, Susan tried to stay <u>connected</u> to Joe by holding his leg. Susan also showed an interest in covering or <u>enveloping</u> the brush with water and face paint, possibly seeing the colour of the water transform when she put the brush back into the water. She chose to <u>envelop</u> her own mouth with red paint, thereby trying out having red lips like Annette.

Joe often brought Susan to nursery. I know from Sian that she and Susan found it painful to separate from each other. I guess that Sian felt that she could protect Susan and herself from some of the pain of that separation by asking Joe to take her. However, I know from my experiences with my own son, that the hidden message might be that the separation is too painful for parent or child to bear, that the pain is too great to be 'contained'. I also know from our discussions, that Sian has had a series of losses, some of which were unresolved at this time. So, while she herself was still experiencing the pain of separation and loss, that pain would be magnified by enduring the pain of separation from Susan each day.

Sian described Susan 'sobbing and not wanting to go to nursery' each day. On a Wednesday, there was no nursery, so each day Susan would 'want to go to town with her mum and granny like on a Wednesday' (discussion with Sian).

That same morning, Susan experimented with lentils and approached Danielle.

Observation: Susan containing lentils and approaching Danielle

Susan walked to the water tray, still carrying the brush. Two other children were playing with lentils and containers. Susan began putting lentils into a container using her hand to scoop them. Callum offered her a container. She did not respond.

Susan noticed that some of the lentils had stuck to her hand. She dropped the brush she was carrying onto the floor. She spooned lentils into a six compartment bun tray and became very involved. Then she picked up handfuls of lentils. Again, she looked at her hand and tried to push the lentils off her hand. She put some lentils into Callum's container, then experimented with putting lentils through a funnel. She pushed some lentils through the funnel. Then she went to the snack area.

Susan to Danielle	*'I'm going to be a witch'.*
Danielle	*'You're going to be a witch tonight?'*
Susan	*'I'm going to a party'.*
Danielle	*'And what's Daniel going to be?'*
Susan	*'Staying at his friend's house'.*

DISCUSSION AND INTERPRETATION OF SUSAN'S ACTIONS AND COMMUNICATION

Using attachment theory to understand Susan's actions, Susan had been in close proximity to Annette for over half an hour. It was as though something else caught her eye and enabled her to leave Annette and to explore in another area of the nursery. What may have been important, was that Annette was now settled and busily face-painting with other children. Susan could see that Annette was still there, so Annette could provide a 'secure base' from which Susan could explore (Bowlby, 1998).

Susan immediately began containing lentils. She did not respond to Callum. By chance, some of them stuck to her hand. She pushed them off – could this have represented her own clinginess? Her action of pushing them off physically separated them from her. A few minutes later, she put some lentils into Callum's <u>container</u>, as though acknowledging his earlier offer.

When Susan went to the snack area, Danielle, her own Family Worker, was there. This was when Susan chose to talk about what was going to be happening at home that evening. Like her mum, she did not have to do a lot of explaining to Danielle. Danielle knew about her context and could have a meaningful conversation with her.

Using schema theory to understand Susan's actions, Susan was very interested in <u>containing</u> the lentils. She became most involved when using a bun tray with six <u>containers</u>, so that she could put lentils into each of the containers and see them divided and <u>contained</u> in an ordered way.

She was also curious when some of the lentils covered or <u>enveloped</u> her hand. The lentils were very different to the face paint that she had used to <u>envelop</u> her mouth earlier. Susan experimented with picking up handfuls and looking at her hands <u>enveloped</u> in lentils, and then pushing them off. She was also fascinated with putting lentils into and <u>through the boundary</u> of a funnel, demonstrating what happened when the lentils were not contained.

Drawing on the psychoanalytic literature, Copley and Forryan (1987, p. 169) described the '"sieve-like" aspect of non-containment, in which a communication seems to run through, rather than into, a mother or maybe a worker; "in one ear and out the other", a kind of pseudo-listening that does not really take in and pay attention'. Perhaps Susan's explorations with the lentils were a representation of her search for a container or containers for her feelings and also a representation of not being heard or understood in relation to those feelings?

Susan's reference to that evening may also have had a link, in the sense that she would be dressed up and transformed into a witch for the party. This involved being <u>enveloped</u> in special clothes and possibly face paints. Daniel, too, would be hidden or <u>enveloped</u> as he would be staying at his friend's house.

Although Susan seemed not to become very involved, when I looked closely, everything she did or said seemed to have significance. She seemed absent-minded when she dropped the brush. It was as though she was not looking for engagement but, occasionally, something caught her attention. Susan seemed slightly out of reach to me, as though she was preoccupied somewhere else. I wondered whether this mirrored Sian's preoccupation with loss.

Throughout the rest of the morning, Susan continued to explore, using different materials.

Observation: Susan exploring and using different materials

Susan manipulated the marble run then walked away saying 'Can't fix it'. I put it back together and she played with it for a few minutes. She was interested in the 'going through' and talked about whether it had a hole or not …

Susan saw another child with dough. Danielle took her to the Wet Area and showed her where the dough was. She picked up a garlic press and manipulated it. I showed her how to open it, put some dough inside, close it and see the dough coming through. She did this several times and said 'It's coming through'. Susan stored the strands of dough in a cup. Susan said 'My mum's got a new dog'. Susan continued putting dough into the garlic press and pressing the handles to make it come through. Once, she used warm, freshly made dough and it came through quickly and easily. I tried to draw her attention to the difference in malleability but she did not seem interested …

Susan experimented with putting lentils through a funnel and sieve, then poured them from lid to pot to bowl and from large spoon to pot to bowl …

DISCUSSION AND INTERPRETATION OF SUSAN'S ACTIONS AND COMMUNICATION

Using attachment theory to understand this sequence of Susan's play, Danielle noticed that Susan was curious about the dough. So Danielle showed her where the dough was available. This was a 'subtle intervention' that enabled Susan to explore and follow her interest (Arnold, 2004; Whalley and Arnold, 1997). Danielle was watching and recognising the subtle signals shown by Susan.

I offered to help twice when I noticed Susan giving up on something, because she did not know how it worked. On both occasions, she sustained her involvement after a little support. Vygotsky would say that I used Susan's 'zone of proximal development' to help her achieve something that day, which she would subsequently be able to achieve alone (Vygotsky, 1978, p. 84). As far as the garlic press was concerned, she practised for almost 30 minutes with very little help. What was interesting was that she did not reject the strands coming through, but stored them in a cup. It was at this point that Susan spoke about her mum having a new dog. This showed that she was thinking about her mum and maybe what was helping her mum to come through a difficult time. Maybe Susan intuitively recognised her new skill with, and interest in, the garlic press as similar to her mum's interest in her new dog.

In this instance Susan seemed to represent 'going through', a process that transformed the whole lump of dough into strands, followed by the provision of a receptacle that contained the strands and in which they could become whole or 'integrated' again.

Using schema theory to understand Susan's play, Susan seemed to have a strong urge to both <u>contain</u> and to put different materials <u>through a boundary</u>. Her interest in whether the marble run had a hole or not showed an understanding of the function of a hole in a container. Obviously, the size of the hole and the malleability of materials defined what went through. Her interest in the garlic press probably added to her knowledge of <u>containing</u> and <u>going through</u>. She was also able to see the material transformed into strands. She closely studied the dough coming through the press and then <u>contained</u> it in a cup.

Subsequently, Susan tried out putting lentils into a funnel, which was quite wide, and then a sieve, with tiny holes. She possibly had experience of water travelling through both of these.

Susan's explorations and involvement with the garlic press indicated that she was interested in 'doing' and in using her new skill competently. Containing the strands of dough in a cup showed that she was also motivated by 'having' or 'holding' things together.

Susan usually wore pink and often the latest fashion. At nursery, she liked wearing special high heels from the dressing-up box. However, she was not fanatical about any of these things. It seemed she could take them or leave them. Perhaps she was different at home where she felt more at ease.

CHANGES

CONTEXT OF THE OBSERVATIONS

During the year I studied Susan, several changes occurred both at home and at nursery. Around November 2003, when Susan was about to become 3, her dad began to visit. She was unsure of him at first and did not want anything to do with him. Her mum's family had mixed feelings about him being back on the scene.

Around the same time, Danielle (Susan's Key Worker) had become pregnant and was often absent due to ill health caused by her pregnancy. Susan could not rely on Danielle being at nursery each day.

In addition to these changes, her mum and family, who Susan saw each day, were still mourning the death of Da, her maternal grandfather, who had died when Susan was 18 months old. Although she could not remember him, his memory was a strong presence within the family.

I have selected the following sequences to try to illuminate how Susan was trying to understand these issues of presence and absence of important people in her family.

In the first observation, Susan was curious about the missing guinea pig.

Observation: Susan was curious about the guinea pig

Susan (2:11:24) had spent several minutes using the drill and saw alongside Annette, when she pointed at a photo of a guinea pig. Annette said 'It went on its holidays and never came back' and then added 'The girl he went to see got fond of him and she doesn't want to return him'.

Five minutes later, Susan knelt on the floor looking at a photo book of workers. She smiled and pointed. 'There's Danielle'. Katey came by and said 'There's Danielle – she's not here today is she?'

Susan spent the next 12 minutes dripping cornflour mix onto her hand and washing it off. She added lentils to the cornflour and washed it off her hand and the spoon repeatedly.

DISCUSSION AND INTERPRETATION OF SUSAN'S ACTIONS AND COMMUNICATION

Using attachment theory to understand, Susan seemed curious first about the guinea pig, whose photo was displayed, but she had never seen. Annette struggled to explain what had happened to the guinea pig. The idea that people go on holiday and never come back, sounded a bit frightening. Annette seemed to realise this and qualified her statement by saying that the guinea pig was with someone who was very fond of him.

Susan possibly sought out photos of Danielle in order to think about her worker, who was away that day. Usually, if a worker was going to be away on holiday or for training, they would talk to the children in their family group about their impending absence and allow each child to choose a substitute Family Worker. Unfortunately, Danielle's absences were unpredictable so she could not prepare the children and no one could say, with certainty, when she would be back, although they could talk about why she was away.

Using schema theory to understand, Susan seemed concerned with covering and uncovering. She repeatedly <u>enveloped</u> her hand and the spoon with cornflour mix and then washed it off. She combined lentils and cornflour and used that mix to <u>envelop</u> her hand and the spoon before washing it off, thereby revealing her hand.

Susan was a lot younger than Sam, who in Chapter 6 articulated her concerns when <u>enveloping</u>. However, given Susan's social context at that time, it seems reasonable to speculate that <u>enveloping</u> and washing off might be connected to understanding about people being here and gone.

I had a sense that Susan was engaging in these sorts of explorations at the time. I now wonder about how often the children had opportunities to talk about absent people, especially when those absences were unpredictable. The photo book was a way of initiating those discussions. Danielle, of all the nursery workers, was open to discussions about loss and death (Arnold, 2004). It may have been helpful for Susan to have photos of her dad and Da at the nursery. Danielle could have helped Susan to understand while everything was still too painful for Sian to talk about.

When Susan's older brother, Daniel, was at the nursery, he used to carry about a book of photos of his important adults from home. This was a tangible way of helping him to 'hold those people in mind' and to talk about them when they were not with him.

It was several months later when Susan (3:5:06) talked about her friend, who had gone to live in Scotland.

Observation: Susan talked about her friend in Scotland

Susan was standing washing her hands at the sink in the bathroom, when she mentioned that her friend, Leah, was on her video. She told me that Leah had gone to live in Scotland.

I asked 'Will you see her again? Isn't Scotland a long way?'

Susan	*'Sharks are at Scotland. They'll eat you'.*
Me	*'Eat you up?'*
Susan	*'Aunty Betty's up there'.*
Me	*'Who told you there's sharks in Scotland?'*
Susan	*'My granny'.*
Me	*'Your granny told you?'*
Susan	*'Yes' (quietly), then (again very quietly) 'Joe told me No' ... 'Joe told me No' (looked amused).*
Me	*'So your friend's not here today?'*
Susan	*'She's at her nursery'.*
Me	*'In Scotland?'*
Susan (nodding)	*'She lives up there'.*
Me	*'Maybe you could write her a letter or send her a photo or something?'*
Me	*'Have you got her address?'*

Susan gave a little nod as she dried her hands and left the bathroom.

DISCUSSION AND INTERPRETATION OF SUSAN'S ACTIONS AND COMMUNICATION

Using attachment theory to understand, Susan was clearly attached to Leah, as a friend. She had memories of being with Leah, that were being kept alive by having Leah on video to remind her of their time together. She also mentioned other important people, Granny, Aunty Betty and Joe. Susan seemed able to understand, at this stage, that granny was teasing her about the sharks in Scotland. She had some evidence, in the sense that she knew some people there, and as far as she knew they had not been eaten by sharks. Anyway Joe had told her there were none. However, there was also a slight tingle of fear and excitement about the fact that there might be 'sharks at Scotland'. Susan was quite animated during this sequence and spoke loudly enough for me to hear, which was often not the case.

Using schema theory to understand, Susan knew that there were images of Leah <u>contained</u> in a video at her house. She could watch that often to remind herself of Leah. The video provided a symbol of Leah. The reference to going to live in Scotland could be conceptualised by Susan, because she had made many journeys in <u>trajectories</u> with stopping off points and a destination (Athey, 1990). Scotland was her friend's destination. Her reference to sharks indicated that <u>inside</u> Scotland, there might be lots of unknown creatures, things to be feared. I made reference to her friend's absence but Susan could conceptualise her friend at her nursery in Scotland, in a different place but possibly doing similar things to her. Susan had generalised her own knowledge about going to nursery to her friend's situation. She could also think about her absence as temporary. Despite the fear of being eaten up or <u>contained</u> by sharks, Susan seemed confident that Leah's absence was not permanent. I suggested sending something (in a <u>trajectory</u>) in order to stay <u>connected</u>, but Susan either was not interested or did not understand the process fully enough to take this up.

I felt so happy to have found some tangible evidence of an increase in Susan's understanding about presence and absence. Sian had obviously talked to Susan at some length about Leah going to live in Scotland. This was probably not possible for Sian when it came to the other losses experienced by her. The loss of Da was possibly too painful still to discuss at length and the losses of her dad and, to some extent, Danielle, were too unpredictable to be able to talk about with any certainty.

There was also the issue of Sian sometimes being too preoccupied with her own grief to be able to respond to Susan's needs fully. Bowlby (1998, p. 43) stated that 'a mother can be physically present but "emotionally" absent' and 'may be unresponsive to her child's desire for mothering'.

Drawing on my personal experiences of loss, I can relate to the all-consuming preoccupation with the loss of a close relative and the feeling of being lost in a kind of haze, with little memory of what is going on in the day-to-day world, and being unresponsive to my children.

In the next two observations, Susan seemed to express some 'ambivalent' feelings when her mum was picking her up from nursery (Bowlby, 1998, p. 41).

SUSAN SHOWING SOME 'AMBIVALENT' FEELINGS

> ## Observation: Reunion with her mother at the water tray
>
> *The children had all been having stories in small groups and those that were staying for lunch were washing their hands in the bathroom. Susan (3:0:25) began playing at the large water tray with a metal bowl, spoons and jugs. There was green water in the tray. She filled the bowl until it overflowed and stirred it with a spoon. Susan looked up and saw Sian, gave a little smile and then looked up almost immediately again, looking a little anxious. She continued adding water to the bowl and stirring and said quietly 'I'm making some cakes for you'. Sian did not quite hear. Susan repeated 'I'm making some cakes' (a bit louder). Susan continued adding water and stirring. She picked up a small ladle and added water with that. Sian said something quietly and repeated 'You should take it out of the bowl'. Susan used the small ladle to scoop some water from the bowl back into the tray, then emptied the bowl and put it down emphatically.*

DISCUSSION AND INTERPRETATION OF SUSAN'S ACTIONS AND COMMUNICATION

Using attachment theory to understand, Susan seemed very much in her own world with the water, 'detached' from other people, although I was close by. She knew that someone would be picking her up but it was not always her mum. She seemed both pleased and a little anxious when her mum came. Maybe she was angry that her mum had left her at nursery and not allowed her to stay at home with her. She may have been a little anxious about whether her mum was all right. She was pleased to see her but continued with her play.

When Susan said 'I'm making cakes for you', she seemed to be inviting her mum into her world. She had to repeat the invitation and said 'I'm making some cakes'. Her mum watched what she was doing and then offered some advice about making cakes. I believe Sian was trying to tune into what Susan was doing and telling her. Both were trying to 'share motives', described by Trevarthen as 'intersubjectivity' (Trevarthen and Aitken, 2001). However, Susan's actions of emptying the bowl and 'putting it down emphatically' suggested to me that she felt a bit angry about her mum's suggestion. She also wanted to please her mum, so the result was a mixed message, which showed some slight 'ambivalence'. Bowlby (1998, p. 293) asserted that 'Thus, love, anxiety, and anger, and sometimes hatred, come to be aroused by one and the same person. As a result painful conflicts are inevitable'. The fact that Susan felt some anger at her mum may have increased her anxiety about her mum. Bowlby (1998, p. 294) pointed out that Klein's work with young children showed that 'some children who are attached to mother with unusual intensity are, paradoxically, possessed of strong unconscious hostility also directed towards her'. Such close relationships can become 'distorted and tangled' (Bowlby, 1998, p. 296).

Using schema theory to understand Susan's actions, Susan was involved in one of her favourite activities, <u>containing</u> water in a bowl, <u>rotating</u> the water with a spoon and allowing it to overflow. When Sian arrived Susan indicated that she was symbolically representing 'making cakes' through co-ordinating her <u>containing</u> and <u>rotation</u> schemas. Sian's suggestion of taking the mixture out of the bowl, prompted Susan to pour the water back into the large water tray and to put the bowl down using a <u>trajectory</u> movement.

I had to watch this sequence many times before I noticed the subtlety of Susan's movement with the bowl. I also have kept asking myself whether there was an alternative interpretation for her actions. I barely noticed the anger and resignation at first, and I do not know whether Sian was aware of those feelings. I was aware of both of them feeling a bit anxious. Those feelings were probably magnified by the public nature of the reunion and by being filmed.

In the next observation, several months later Susan was at grouptime with Kerri, her new Family Worker, who was covering Danielle's maternity leave.

▨ CONTEXT OF OBSERVATION

The following observation was made a few days after Sian's birthday and the second anniversary of Da's death. This was a difficult time for Sian. It could also have been a difficult time for Susan. We were aware that several children, with whom Susan was familiar, would be leaving the nursery and we wanted to prepare Susan for those changes. Susan would be coming to the nursery for four full days. We introduced her to the dining room where she would be having lunch at the nursery and she chose where and with whom she would like to sit each day. She chose to sit next to Angela, Head of Nursery, who subsequently became important to Susan.

Observation: Susan enveloping play people and being reunited with her mum

While the children were waiting to begin their grouptime, Susan (3:7:26) was manipulating a piece of cloth and two play people, a male and female figure. She wrapped the play people in the cloth. When Kerri was ready to begin the story, she asked Susan to give her the play people. Susan gave Kerri the play people but continued to manipulate the cloth placing it on her knee, under her feet and generally keeping contact with it.

At the end of grouptime while the other children were washing their hands, Kerri was putting Susan's shoes on her and talking about the fact that some children were going to leave nursery and go to big school soon. Susan and Robert would stay for another year and some new children would start.

Susan got up and walked over to the table where the two play people were lying. She wrapped them in the cloth once again and went towards the entrance. As she stepped across the threshold, she noticed her mum waiting for her on the arm of a chair. She quite deliberately tossed the cloth containing the play people a couple of inches into the air and allowed it to drop on the floor.

> *She looked down at the play people and walked to her mum with her arms out-stretched. She placed her hands on her mum's arms. Her mum 'danced' Susan's hands up and down, then asked 'Where's your jacket?' Susan pointed back to where she had come from. Sian asked her 'Do you remember Rosanna?' indicating the person sitting on the chair.*

DISCUSSION AND INTERPRETATION OF SUSAN'S ACTIONS AND COMMUNICATION

Using attachment theory to understand, it seemed significant that Susan was playing with two figures that might represent her mum and dad or her mum and her Da. Sian was feeling low that week. Putting two adult dolls together might have represented Susan's wish to have her dad or Da back and for her mum to be happy in a relationship with one or other, or even both of them. However, if her dad or Da were back, she might not feel as close to her mum. Susan may have been feeling ambivalent because she wanted her mum to be happy and have the people she wanted with her, but also she wanted to be special to her mum.

She approached her mum with open arms but Sian did not mirror the wide arm movement but kept her arms closed with her hands resting on her legs. Maybe Sian was anxious about how Susan had been that morning, unable to be open to Susan's feelings because she, herself, was feeling sad and over-whelmed? Susan rested her hands on her mum's arms and then Sian held her hands and 'danced' them up and down. Sian also diverted Susan's attention from their reunion by asking where her jacket was and then asking if Susan remembered Rosanna. I think Sian may have been scared to take on Susan's feelings.

Kerri was helping Susan to know about and to understand the imminent loss of some of her friends to school. She did this by explaining who would be leaving, who would be staying and that some new children would be joining their group at nursery. Kerri was preparing Susan for other small losses and changes she would endure during the next couple of months. This conversation may have disturbed Susan too.

Using schema theory to understand, Susan <u>enveloped</u> or <u>contained</u> the two play people in the cloth, possibly to keep them safe or to keep them together. Separating had caused her mum to feel sad, so her natural action might be to represent people together. Susan also sustained contact with the cloth, which, like her comfort cloths might provide comfort. It was soft and pliable and could be a 'defence against anxiety' (Winnicott, 1975, p. 232).

Her 'toss' of the cloth containing the two play people was an upward <u>trajectory</u> resulting in the play people inside the cloth falling in a downward <u>trajectory</u>. She looked down at them but left them behind once her mum was there. Was she rejecting her fantasy that her mum and dad or Da could be reunited?

I have felt for some time that this sequence was significant. Susan looked so sad and moved so slowly that the whole scenario has always had a sad feel to it. I realised that I was scared of understanding what it might mean. I was keen that Susan was rejecting the play people because she did not need them, because her mum was there to comfort her. However, I was disregarding Sian's feelings, expecting her to be responsive when she was actually feeling very low herself and therefore unable to be open to accepting Susan's feelings or to publicly express her own feelings. What she may have been feeling was a whole mixture of relief (that Susan was all right), emptiness (about the anniversary of Da's death) and embarrassment (about being filmed at this difficult time). Sian used distraction to divert everyone's attention away from the very pain she was enduring.

Perhaps through our preparation for Susan's friends leaving, we had an opportunity to help her identify her feelings, that is by articulating, 'You might feel sad when they go but you will make some new friends ...'? Susan needed some experiences of feeling sad about losses and being able to talk about and express her feelings. She needed to have her feelings 'contained' by another person and returned to her in a manageable form so that she could acknowledge those feelings and bear them (Bion, 1962).

WHAT HAPPENED DURING THE FOLLOWING YEAR

During the following year, Susan continued to explore <u>containment</u> using various materials. She also learned to ride a two-wheeler bike. She became close to Angela (Head of Nursery), who became something of an advocate for Susan. For Susan's fourth birthday, Susan and Sian went to Disneyland Paris for four days, just the two of them. Susan brought her photos of the trip into nursery. Susan was most excited about Cinderella, who was 'in a carriage, a pumpkin, a pumpkin, a pumpkin', a <u>container</u> transformed by magic into a carriage for the Princess (Prodger, 2005).

I have focused on a small number of observations to tell one possible story about Susan and her explorations. There was further evidence in the data gathered, that Susan was very interested in <u>containing</u> various materials in different containers. She continued and extended these explorations for another year at nursery, before moving on to primary school.

Sam (Chapter 6) was described as having an 'other world' quality about her. Susan seemed to be in her 'own world'. It was difficult to get close to her and to try to work out what she was thinking and feeling. In some ways, she seemed self-contained. Angela worked hard at getting close to Susan during her second year at nursery. Susan began to trust Angela and to be more relaxed around her, to tease and joke a little, as she might have done with members of the extended family at home.

SO WHAT?

Studying Susan brought emotional issues to the forefront for me. There will always be children in settings who are suffering emotionally because of issues in their families. The danger with quiet children, like Susan, is that they can so easily be unheard. Listening to each child and their many communications is vital for us, as parents and workers.

Responding to emotional needs, does not mean ignoring children's cognitive needs. Susan had the same right to a challenging curriculum as any other child and sometimes that can be lost when children's and families' needs are being responded to in settings. In fact, Susan may have been using her cognition to give form to her emotions, for example, when exploring <u>going through a boundary</u>.

In this instance, it was also helpful and important to know something of the family history and to be in touch with Sian's needs. Our work in early childhood settings is always concerned with children and their families and building close relationships can enable us to understand family issues. It was worthwhile to engage in dialogue with Sian about Susan. Through talking about Susan's ambivalence towards her, Sian recognised the ambivalence she feels towards her mother.

Table 7.1 Schemas mentioned and links made

Enveloping	Susan seemed to envelop objects and parts of her body to symbolise 'here and gone'
Containing	Susan was interested in containing materials. She seemed to want to keep things together e.g. dough when it came through the garlic press
Going through a boundary	Susan explored this pattern with different materials. She seemed to seek out sieves, funnels etc. that enabled her to explore 'going through' in different ways
Connecting	Susan tried to stay connected to Joe and subsequently attached herself to Annette
Trajectory	Susan could reflect on her friend Leah's journey to go and live in Scotland. We deduced that her understanding was based on many early journeys she had made, with stopping off points
Inside	Susan could talk about and think about her friend, Leah, inside the video she had and also inside a place called Scotland
Rotating	Susan liked to mix and stir using a rotating action to 'make cakes'

SUGGESTED FURTHER READING

Athey, C. (1990) *Extending Thought in Young Children*, Paul Chapman, London.

Athey, C. (2007) *Extending Thought in Young Children*, 2nd edn, Paul Chapman, London.

Bowlby, J. (1998) *Attachment and Loss Volume 2*, Pimlico, London.

Copley, B. and Forryan, B. (1987) *Therapeutic Work with Children and Young People*, Cassell, Trowbridge.

Meade, A. and Cubey, P. (2008) *Thinking Children: Learning About Schemas*, Open University Press, Maidenhead.

Wickes, F.G. (1978) *The Inner World of Childhood*, Sigo Press, Boston, MA. First published in 1927.

8

Cara: Trying to Make Sense of a Death in her Family

This chapter introduces:

- Cara and her family
- Two observations of Cara made shortly after her great uncle's death
- One observation made three weeks later

INTRODUCTION AND CONTEXT

Cara was one of the children involved in the wider study of children's emotional well-being and resilience, being undertaken by a team of researchers at the Pen Green Research Base from 2000 to 2004. Although Cara and her family were not the focus of this study, I wanted to report on three linked observations of Cara, made around the time of her great uncle's death. I think that these observations offer some insights into how Cara was feeling and trying to understand what had happened.

Cara's extended family are very well known to me as they have been regularly using the centre since it opened 26 years ago. Cara's mum and her brother and sister all attended the nursery. Her grandmother runs parent groups and has been a crèche worker. Her granddad regularly uses the centre. Cara is the eldest of three children and the first to attend nursery in her immediate family.

Despite all of our knowledge of the family and their agreement to being part of the study, 'gathering video observations of Cara was problematic' (Pen Green Team, 2004, p. 111). Cara would often avoid the camera or look uncomfortable. Twice the researcher asked Cara if she wanted her to stop filming and she said 'Yes'. On other occasions, the researcher stopped filming because Cara looked uncomfortable.

Through discussions with her Key Worker, Michelle, we established that Cara was 'very interested in <u>envelopment</u>. She usually worked at a sensori-motor level, enjoying the feeling of the materials, and seeming to 'lose' herself in the experience'. Cara also sought out 'one to one contact with adults' (Pen Green Team, 2004, p. 111). In fact, twice she had sought me out to read a book called *No Worries* to her.

Another significant feature was that during the three years of her life, the family had lived in various locations: at their gran and granddad's house, in temporary housing and now in their own flat. So there had been lots of changes and transitions for Cara to cope with. This also meant that her parents were not able to become very involved in the study.

The first two observations were made on the same day:

CONTEXT OF FIRST OBSERVATION

We had arranged to film Cara for 30 minutes during the morning. She seemed fairly unfocused at first, but did become 'involved' in a sort of 'losing' herself way with the cornflour. She stayed at the cornflour for ten minutes.

Observation: Manipulating cornflour

Cara (4:0:26) approached the table in the Messy Area where two other children and an adult were playing with a mixture of pink cornflour and water. Cara dipped her finger in and then seemed to decide to explore further. She pushed her sleeves up and went to the side of the table where no one else was standing. Cara got a large spoon from the tray of cornflour and tried to pick up some of the mixture. The adult said 'I like to do this Cara – scoop it up'. The adult held a spatula in the air with cornflour dripping from it. Cara grasped some of the mix in her hand and watched it drip and stretch from her hand onto the tray below.

Adult	*'Does that feel good? What does it feel like?'*
Cara	*'Pink'.*
Adult	*'It is pink'.*

Cara continued looking for the pouring property, sometimes squeezing the mix into a ball in her hand before opening her hand and letting it drip. She used a spoon again to scoop some of the mix up and poured it from spoon to hand and back to spoon. She pushed her hands into the mix on the tray and stared. She picked up a lump of mix and let it drip onto her wrist and showed the observer. She put her hand into a container being used by a little boy nearby. He said 'Stop it, Cara!' Then Cara picked up a paintbrush and made some side to side movements with the brush, 'sweeping' the mix that had dripped onto the table.

The boy moved away and Cara immediately moved around to that side of the table, picked up the small container he had been using and poured the mix from that into a larger bowl already containing some of the mix. Then she poured from the large bowl back into the small container and some of the mix overflowed. The adult was talking about making pudding. When the cornflour overflowed, the adult talked about 'picking it up and scooping it back into the large tray'. Cara continued to attend to the cornflour dripping. She held her small container under the edge of the table to catch the drips. The phone rang and Cara's ears pricked. The adult noticed and said 'Are you thinking about it?' (Meaning the phone I think.) Cara moved away, washed her hands and went to use the computer.

DISCUSSION AND INTERPRETATION OF CARA'S ACTIONS AND COMMUNICATION

Using attachment theory to understand, Cara seemed not to connect very much with the other children or the adult at the cornflour table. She seemed detached and in her own world, as though she was preoccupied with something and just going through the motions of playing with the cornflour. The play seemed to have a therapeutic feel to it. Laevers's definition of 'involvement' includes exploration and Cara did not seem to be looking for anything new at this time (Laevers, 1997). However there was a sort of 'involvement' in the here and now feel of the cornflour. Perhaps involvement is not the right term to use. She may have been returning to the 'known' or 'familiar' (Jackson, 2004, p. 55) in order to wallow or remain 'held together' by doing something very familiar to her. The phone ringing cut in though and she perked up as though she thought it might be for her.

Using schema theory to understand Cara's explorations, she gave most attention to the changing state of the cornflour, its _transformation_. She obviously understood the properties well, having played with cornflour and water many times before. She was interested in <u>containing</u> the mix in a spoon, in her hand and then in a container and watching the transformation when she released the mix by pouring. This was important because she was bringing about that 'transformation' through her actions (Athey, 1990, p. 29). What was surprising was that she poured the mix from a large container into a smaller one and it overflowed, but perhaps this mirrored her own feelings on that day.

I remember discussing Cara's lack of involvement with my colleague, who filmed the sequences of Cara. Cara was one of those children who was interested in the camera and in what could be seen through the lens. It was rare for her to forget about the camera and, every now and then, she asked to see herself on the little screen that could be turned towards her.

The way Cara responded to the phone suggested to me that she was preoccupied with thinking about home, marking or passing time until she could return. She showed no distress but was certainly not like a 'fish in water' on that occasion (Laevers, 1997). I have also reflected on the properties of the cornflour mix, which are fascinating even to an adult. It is a solid when squeezed together and becomes a liquid when released, so, unlike most materials, nothing is added or taken away in order to transform the mix from a solid to a liquid form.

CONTEXT OF SECOND OBSERVATION

Within the next few minutes, Cara dabbled with the computer, then did some drawing on the flipchart (two very small <u>enclosures</u> in one corner of a big piece of paper), then did some cutting at the writing table. Eventually she began to listen to Danielle, a worker, who was with some other children in the corridor, a quieter area than where Cara was playing with the cornflour. Danielle was a worker, who we had identified as being open to and often in tune with children's emotional needs (Arnold, 2004). It may not have been a coincidence that Cara approached Danielle on a day when Cara was feeling confused and unsure. Danielle was kneeling on the floor and saying to Susan, 'You could take that home and show your granny'.

Observation: Interacting with Danielle

Cara came across Danielle in the corridor with other children, looking at their Special Books. She found a photo book of her own family and had a conversation with Danielle about her granny feeling sad and staying at home that day because her granny's brother had died.

Cara wanted to know why her granny was sad and why her great uncle had died. Danielle responded that her granny was sad because her brother had died and that she did not know why he had died.

Danielle was also able to make a connection for Susan, who said 'My mum's friend's brother died' by pointing out that Susan's mum's friend and Cara's granny are sisters and both were feeling sad because their brother had died.

Danielle and Cara looked through the photo book twice, talking about Cara's family and remembering happier times.

DISCUSSION AND INTERPRETATION OF CARA'S ACTIONS AND COMMUNICATION

Using attachment theory to understand this sequence, Cara seemed to find a container for her feelings in Danielle (Bion, 1962). She was able to tell Danielle what was worrying and preoccupying her on this day. Danielle was not only receptive, but had enough knowledge of Cara's family context to know about what had happened and to be able to help Cara gain a coherent understanding of why her granny was sad. Danielle was also authentic and honest in that she responded to Cara's question 'Why?' with 'I don't know'. Cara's grandparents are Scottish and so is Danielle, so Danielle was able to 'tune into' Cara's concern with a speech rhythm that may have been familiar as well as a tone that expressed genuine concern. Danielle never closed down the conversation. It went two ways and Danielle was prepared to listen. The photo book was invaluable, as a way in to talk about what had happened, and as a comfort and to remind Cara of happier times and of times when she was physically close to members of her immediate family. Somehow, Danielle seemed to achieve a perfect balance between allowing for Cara's feelings to be expressed and empathising, and being distant enough to be able to talk about her great uncle's death. That might have been hard for Cara's granny or mother to do so soon after his death. Hare et al. (1986, p. 51) reported that 'fear and anxiety about death can prevent teachers from openly talking to children about their loss. Such a "conspiracy of silence" may quickly be translated by bereaved children to mean that whatever feelings they may have in response to the death must be suppressed'.

Using schema theory to understand Cara's actions, she seemed to be moving around the nursery in a <u>trajectory</u> with stopping off points, searching for something to engage with. I imagine she was feeling confused and not fully understanding why she had to come to nursery, while her granny stayed at home. Several times Danielle referred to or asked about the <u>connections</u> between the people in the photos. Cara was able to explain those connections, for example 'She's my cousin'. In a way, the narrative constructed through looking at her photo book provided some sort of 'container' for Cara's confusion. Holmes described a coherent narrative as something which 'creates out of fragmentary experience an unbroken line or thread linking the present with the past and future', a kind of joined up <u>trajectory</u> (Holmes, 1993, p. 150).

I suppose what was captured on film here, was something that happened quite naturally for Danielle and Cara. No special preparations were made to help Cara talk about her great uncle's death, as far as I know. I cannot help thinking that it was no coincidence that eventually, on that day, Cara found Danielle. Before that, she was searching, unengaged and seemed unfocused. Unfortunately, we do not know whether she settled down for the rest of the day after her conversation with Danielle. Maybe she stayed near Danielle, who understood something of what she was feeling? I am reminded of Juliet Hopkin's work with nursery nurses, who came to the realisation that if they picked up a distressed child and allowed them to have a good cry, they then became much more settled than if they used 'distraction' (Hopkins, 1988, p. 104).

■ CONTEXT OF THIRD OBSERVATION

Just over three weeks after her great uncle's death, I was filming another child, who approached her Family Worker, Margaret, in the corridor. Margaret was working with Cara, recording a story Cara was telling her. Margaret sensed that it was important to Cara to finish her story before responding to the other child. I waited alongside the other child and continued filming.

> ### Observation: Telling a story to Margaret
>
> *Cara (4:1:19) was drawing and, at the same time, telling a story. Margaret repeated her words back to her and asked questions to clarify what Cara meant. This was the story: 'There was a little mouse and it died … I'm making a gun … the gun that died the mouse … and Cara with scribbles on me and I've done the fire.' (Cara showed Margaret the shooting action and fire coming out of the gun towards the mouse which she drew.)*

DISCUSSION AND INTERPRETATION OF CARA'S ACTIONS AND COMMUNICATION

Using attachment theory to understand Cara's story, it seemed no coincidence that three weeks after experiencing the effects of a death in the family, Cara was exploring death in a story. Rather than thinking about the proximity of people important to her, Cara was placing herself as a central character in a story about the death of a mouse. Anthony (1940, p. 45) reported that the idea of 'death as the result of aggression' was one of two typical responses in young children to death. The other, she described as 'sorrowful separation'. Death was typically seen by children as 'a fear-bringing thing' (in the case of aggression) and a 'sorrow-bringing thing'. Within my own experience, one storytime when we were chatting, one child asked about my dad. I said 'He died a long time ago'. One little boy asked 'Who killed him?' Perhaps young children experience 'killing' in stories and on television, alongside dying and therefore treat them as synonymous.

Using schema theory, Cara clearly articulated by drawing, gesticulating and using language the <u>trajectory</u> of the fire travelling from the gun to the mouse. She used 'died' as a transitive verb, showing that her use of the word 'die' was synonymous with 'kill'. Margaret reflected back to her 'You've done the bullet flying from you to the mouse'. Margaret made a side to side arm movement as she said this. Cara's drawing looked like a scribble but what she was trying to represent was the movement from the gun to the mouse, with the idea of 'fire' that makes a kind of <u>central core with radials</u> coming out of it.

It was sheer chance that I filmed this brief sequence but I did think that it was significant in terms of Cara's understanding. To make a connection between dying and her previous experiences, Cara reached back to her experience of the action of the pulling of a trigger and releasing fire from a gun, something she had seen, probably on television, and that resulted in someone dying. Perhaps in her mind, the mouse dying was 'functionally dependent' on the action of a person.

Perhaps this was what I will refer to as 'reflective expansion'? (See the final chapter for a full explanation of this concept.) Cara literally sought a connection and expanded something from her previous experiences to help her begin to explore and to understand the concept of death. I can only wonder what sense she was making of her great uncle's death. Even as adults, we talk about people being 'struck down' by an illness as though it was done with intent.

DRAWING THE THREE OBSERVATIONS TOGETHER

I have drawn on three observations of Cara to demonstrate what happened around the time of a death in her extended family. In the first observation, she seemed to seek comfort in manipulating a mix of cornflour and water. She did not, as I suspected, <u>envelop</u> objects or herself with the cornflour as I had observed other children do, when trying to understand 'here and gone' or loss of some kind. What she seemed to be interested in was the transformative properties of the cornflour and the overwhelmingness of a large amount put into a small container.

In the second observation, she sought containment for her confusion and sadness about not being able to be near her granny while her granny was feeling sad. Maybe seeing her granny sad was new to Cara, a transformation of a kind. Danielle was able to allow the emotional space for Cara and to offer her comfort and some understanding of her granny's sadness.

In the final observation, three weeks later, Cara expressed some of her ideas about death in her drawing and storytelling. She talked about a little mouse dying. Her ideas about death and dying were transferred to the mouse, which may have felt less threatening to Cara.

SO WHAT?

We learned a great deal from observing Cara and Danielle. Aspects that might be useful to other parents and workers were:

- Danielle's sheer knowledge of and interest in each child and who are important people for each child enabled them to have an authentic conversation about a difficult subject.

- Danielle's openness to difficult and distressing material, which Cara may have sensed, also made it possible for Cara to share her worries.

- Use of photo books to help children to talk about their family and any anxiety about family members.

Margaret, too, was supportive and ready to:

- Record Cara's story word for word and to understand Cara's depiction of the story, which probably helped Cara to give form to her thoughts and feelings. The process of recording Cara's story also helped the adults (family and workers) to understand what Cara was struggling to understand both cognitively and emotionally.

Table 8.1 Schemas mentioned and links made

Enveloping	Cara did not seem to use enveloping to represent 'here and gone' as we have seen other children do
Transformation	Cara was interested in the transformation of the cornflour from a solid to a liquid state and from liquid back to solid state
Containing	Cara seemed interested in containing the cornflour in a spoon, her hand and other containers
Enclosing	Cara drew two small enclosures on a large sheet of paper
Trajectory	Cara moved around with stopping-off points, connected the past with the present and future through reflecting on her 'family book' and represented a bullet going from a gun to a mouse in her drawing
Core with radials	Cara drew a core with radials to symbolically represent 'fire' from a gun

SUGGESTED FURTHER READING

Anthony, S. (1940) *The Child's Discovery of Death*, Routledge, London.

Athey, C. (1990) *Extending Thought in Young Children*, Paul Chapman, London.

Athey, C. (2007) *Extending Thought in Young Children*, 2nd edn, Paul Chapman, London.

9

The Inside Story: An Early Years Practitioner Studying Children's Emotions

It is one's inner experiences that permit gaining a full grasp of what is involved in the inner experiences of others, a knowledge which can then become the basis for theoretical studies. (Bettelheim, 1956/1990, p. 38)

This chapter introduces:

- The emotional experience of studying the relational experiences of young children

- 'Containment' experienced through discussions with colleagues

- Reflecting through keeping a learning journal

- Two themes around my responses to emotions

INTRODUCTION AND CONTEXT

When I embarked on a study of young children's emotions, I was warned that it would be emotionally challenging and painful. At one level, I understood that, as a mature worker with a grown up family, the material might put me in touch with how I parented my children and how I was parented by my parents. At another level, it came as something of a shock. My new awareness and deeply felt emotions crept up on me and sometimes took me by surprise.

At the start of the study, I intended abandoning my earlier interest in schema theory in favour of the psychoanalytic literature, that I was sure would give me some new insights into the children's emotional development. I did not realise how difficult I would find replacing one deep interest with another. I found myself floundering with no firm knowledge base on which to build an authentic study. I will always be grateful for a 10-minute chance conversation I had one day in the library at the Pen Green Research Base. A visiting professor asked me how my study was going and, within 10 minutes, I had decided to use my curiosity about why young children explore particular schemas extensively over time as the basis of my investigation. Up until then, I had automatically applied schema theory to any observations made of children I was studying. I then tried to resist using schema theory and experimented with and practised using several other frameworks from the literature, for example, Judy Dunn's work on 'close relationships' and Bowlby's theory of 'attachment'.

I was really struggling. I wondered whether I was finding the theory too new (to me)? Or was it unrelated to what I felt I knew about? Or did I resist because I unconsciously wanted to avoid getting in touch with painful feelings from my own childhood?

◀ Me with my mum

Me as a mother for
the first time ▶

Isca Wittenberg has written about the 'emotional experience of teaching and learning'. She says:

> What the psycho-analytic study of the mind has shown is that experiences right from the beginning of life, and in fact the earlier back they go the more powerful their influence, remain with us in the depths of the mind throughout our lives, and are re-voked in any situation that in any way resembles the past. (1999, p. 7)

Perhaps the novelty of applying new theory to observations of the children was (r)evoking anxieties in me connected to other new experiences very early in my childhood.

I was aware of a whole body of research on infant observation, as practised at the Tavistock Clinic in London. This is well documented and I had read about this method, described by Miller et al. (1989, p. 2): 'This method of infant observation attempts to take emotion into account. A new concept of the observer is being employed ... here the truths which interest us are themselves emotional truths.'

The purpose of this kind of observational technique, used when observing babies and young children, is to 'stir' up the emotions in the observer. Miller et al. point out that 'correctly grasped, the emotional factor is an indispensable tool to be used in the service of greater understanding' (1989, p. 3).

Peter Elfer has pioneered the use of this type of observation in nursery settings over the last 10 years (Elfer, 1996, 2003). He reports on the method: 'It is more that the observer learns to make her or himself emotionally open to what can be *felt* as well as *seen and heard* during the observation' (2003, p. 5, original emphasis). How could I study young children's emotions without being open to *feeling* them?

Elfer goes on to describe an important part of the process:

> All of this information, the tiny details of what has been noticed, the hunches and feelings that have been evoked, has then to be carefully 'unpicked' by a wider group of experienced observers who can begin to form first ideas about what meaning it might reveal about how the baby is thinking and feeling. (2003, p. 5)

The Tavistock Method involves close observation, openness to what is felt and discussion of the meaning in a regular small group.

It was not my intention, at the outset, to try out this method. I had always tried to emulate the work of Susan Isaacs, and had practised presenting the language and actions I had observed without judgement initially (1930, 1933). When studying different methods or styles of observation, I found myself quite irritated when the voice of the observer intruded and sometimes seemed to detract from what was being observed. For example, in some of the

Learning Stories from New Zealand, the worker's enthusiasm is sometimes expressed as part of the Learning Story. Some workers speak directly to the child they are observing and begin with, for example, 'Wow'! I found that this enthusiasm grated on me a little.

Margaret Carr (2001, p. 97) describes the 'shift from deficit to credit' and I would wholeheartedly support this approach to assessing children's learning. However, on my visit to New Zealand I found some of the words used by workers a little strong and always very positive. I suppose within that positivity, for me, there was a sort of falseness, what Winnicott might refer to as a 'false self' (2006, p. 95). I got the feeling that workers always had to display positivity regardless of how they were feeling, and maybe the hidden message to children was that they, too, should always display positive feelings. I tried to unpick my discomfort with the extreme use of this approach. I concluded that my discomfort must have been rooted in my own upbringing in which there was little space for expressing anger or sadness. I think, in Susan Isaacs, I found an authentic voice. Her focus was not on the adult's feelings but, as an adult, she acted in a very 'matter of fact' way and readily acknowledged all of the interests and feelings of the children. This acceptance and authenticity was important for my learning.

What I found most helpful in the process of reflecting on the observations were:

- my discussions with colleagues

- keeping a learning journal.

In this chapter I have drawn on material from my discussions and from my journal to illustrate some insights I gained over time.

DISCUSSIONS WITH COLLEAGUES

These discussions came in different forms, some planned and others more spontaneous. As a small research team, we engaged in regular discussions about the observations. I cannot overemphasise the importance of these regular meetings (monthly at least). The small team, whom I trusted, provided a 'container' for my feelings, by listening and reassuring me that it was acceptable to express my pain when I began to get in touch with some of my more painful feelings about some observations. Shuttleworth (1994, p. 305) described Bion's concept of 'containment' as a function that parents carry out with their infants,

> Bion felt that a baby who was overwhelmed by distress was in a state which could not of itself become a meaningful experience – rather there

was a tendency for the baby's physical and psychic state to deteriorate and the baby's rudimentary capacity for a coherent sense of himself to be lost. The infant then requires the intervention of a more mature personality – an adult who could tolerate the feelings which the distressed baby arouses.

Shuttleworth went on to explain that 'this gives the baby his first contact with the human capacity for bearing pain through thinking' (1994, p. 306). So talking things through in the group helped me to think things through and, therefore, understand and bear the pain of my new awareness.

I also had monthly meetings with my work supervisor, who was open to discussing my feelings, as well as the observations of the children. In addition I met fairly regularly with my study supervisor, also with Chris Athey (an expert on schemas), and occasionally with Colwyn Trevarthen and Julia Formosinho (both eminent researchers in the field of relationships). Ironically, none of these people could offer the sort of clinical supervision that I would recommend to others embarking on this sort of work. In a way, I used the team and my close colleagues to help me make sense of what was happening. I also kept a learning journal throughout this process.

KEEPING A LEARNING JOURNAL

I kept a journal of anything that occurred to me, after observing the children directly, or after discussions with workers or parents or when revisiting video observations. Sometimes I woke up in the morning with a new thought and went straight to my journal. The real learning was so elusive that I struggled to grasp it and was afraid of losing my grasp on any aspect of it. A lot of the time, I could not work out where my thoughts or ideas had come from. When I got stuck, I often went to the theory and reading often stimulated something in me. I enjoyed recording my thoughts. It felt like an unfolding story, getting something off my chest, a relief almost. Janesick (2000, p. 392) described 'The act of journal writing' as 'a rigorous documentary tool'. The act of writing gave form to my thoughts and feelings. This was where most of my new learning was situated during this study.

Ellis and Bochner (2000, p. 741) explained that there was a shift in the 1970s 'from an emphasis on participant observation to the "observation of participation" and to an emphasis on the process of writing'. They went on to point out that some researchers, when writing of their personal experiences, 'wrote under pen names to avoid losing academic credibility' (2000, p. 741). This raises the idea of what we value as knowledge and research. There could be a danger of being indulgent. However, I have been mindful of this and I do not see myself as the central character in this tale of action. What I have attempted is to tell the 'inside story' alongside and of equal value to each child's story I have presented.

THE INSIDE STORY

The themes that emerged from my learning journal were:

- My tendencies to minimise and avoid emotions and emotional issues.

- Using language to distance myself from emotions.

Although, ostensibly I was studying children's emotions and emotional lives, most of my 'defenses' were employed in avoiding conflict situations and therefore in avoiding intense emotions (Fonagy, 1999, p. 601).

MINIMISING AND AVOIDING EMOTIONS AND EMOTIONAL ISSUES

I had been studying young children's cognition for a number of years (Arnold, 1990, 1997) and only occasionally considering their emotions (Arnold, 1999, 2003), when I took up the opportunity to study children's emotions as a main focus.

Using similar methods to those I had used before, I embarked on the study of a small number of children. I used a tried and tested methodology, using filmed sequences of the children involved in play in the nursery as a basis for discussions with their parents and workers (Jordan and Henderson, 1995; Whalley, 2001; Whalley and Arnold, 1997). First, I tried to ignore the cognitive aspects of development but found this impossible. I needed to go from what I knew into the less known (Formosinho, 2003). I found myself less comfortable discussing the children's emotional development than I had been previously discussing cognitive development. I was happy to listen but did not want to appear critical or to offer advice to the parents. We had discovered a way of sharing child development theory with parents, that enabled us to have an 'equal and active dialogue' about their children (Whalley, 2001). I knew a little about 'attachment theory' (Bowlby, 1998) but, at the outset, was not able to use language about attachment confidently.

My learning journal shows that I frequently felt lost, that some of the ideas I was reading about seemed slightly out of my grasp at first. Occasionally, something a parent said or did surprised me and made me think more deeply.

> ## Journal entry
>
> *Met with M on Thursday and looked at J at Dance. Realised that M does not really understand why she needs to say 'Goodbye' to her children and go. I talked about J being able to feel the pain of the goodbye (loss) and survive and the role of the parents in 'containing' those feelings for J. I wonder whether I need to illustrate the concept in some other way?? Would a better explanation help me and the parents to understand better??*

DISCUSSION

This was a parent I had worked with over a number of years and who had had three children attend the nursery. I realised that I could not have been clear or explicit with her about concepts like 'attachment' and 'containment' if she was still unclear. This parent had a good understanding of schemas and other key child development concepts we had shared with her.

I felt I had probably avoided saying things that I found difficult to voice about her child and his attachment status to her. I wanted my relationship with her to be positive but, actually, her relationship with her child was much more important than mine with her. My duty, as a practitioner, was to her child.

Also, there was a parallel process here. If I could not bear to say difficult things to her about the theory of attachment and how it related to her and her child, then I was like a parent trying to shelter a child from pain. I was not feeling sufficiently competent to 'contain' or 'hold' her feelings of distress, just as she may not have been feeling able or seen that it was necessary to do the same for her child. Maybe my feelings about my child or the child in me were not being contained and, therefore, I could not risk containing her feelings (Bion, 1962). Shaw (1991, p. 132) found that 'a critical discussion of the research with a psychologist within a psychoanalytic framework' helped her to 'appreciate the meaning perspectives of the research participants'. I was probably realising that I needed another supervisor, who could help me to apply a psychoanalytic framework to the research material. It seemed no coincidence that I had carefully chosen a team of supervisors, who were highly qualified in considering the cognitive and sociological perspectives of my study, but no one from the field of psychoanalysis. Perhaps I was avoiding emotions.

If I could use the strategy we had developed, of sharing concepts with the parents, then I would be taking on a different role, not criticising, but sharing information which would enable the parent to make sense of what was happening in much the same way as I was doing. If this was not safe for me, how could I make it safe for the parents?

> ## Journal entry
>
> *Had a tutorial with Chris. She is trying to get me focused on collecting the rest of the data and the questions I want to address. I know that I need to reduce the data and I want to involve the parents in deciding which segments we focus on. Her suggestion is to have a kind of 'clip log' so that parents could choose which bits to focus on. I also need prompts. It might be better if I raise the kind of questions I am interested in and share them with the parents.*

▨ DISCUSSION

At this stage, I was drowning in data and so were the parents. They had seen all of the video material on their own children and, for them, it was a good record to keep of their child at the nursery. On reflection, I decided it was my job to select the sequences for deep analysis. I think I was trying to shift the responsibility for which sequences to consider onto the parents. If any painful discussions ensued, then that conflict was not my doing. I needed someone who would 'contain' my feelings if I was to risk giving my interpretation to the parents (Bion, 1962).

In the end I needed to 'cut to the chase' and be brave about what I selected and the story that the data told (Fletcher, 2006). The parents could offer a different interpretation but, mostly, I made sense of the data through what the parents had told me about their current family situations and contexts.

> ## Journal entry
>
> *Spent all day yesterday looking at and copying six sequences of C. Began summarising them on a chart as discussed with Chris, so that A (her mother) could choose what to focus on. I get excited and animated when watching but then in the summarising find myself recording the action with objects rather than the relationships. I actually begin to put information about relationships on a separate sheet of paper and place that underneath the information about C's actions with objects. I think I am minimising the importance of what goes on within the relationships as I am fearful? Or cannot understand?? Or am less interested?*

▨ DISCUSSION

This was a very strange experience, as though I was looking in on my actions from the outside and realising that, for me, cognition was 'on top'. (There was also a fear.) My fear was that I was not seeing or considering the whole child, with thoughts and feelings but was ignoring affect by having a strong focus on cognition. Was my long-standing focus on and interest in cognition a 'defense' against emotions?

Journal entry

I had a very strange experience this morning. A couple of weeks ago I made a short video about E – distressed separation followed by connecting behaviour then more connecting a year later. I gave Annette (worker) and A (his mum) a copy each. I asked permission to use it in training. Annette suggested that we use it on the MA to illustrate our well-being project. I hadn't heard from A, so I nipped across the road at 3 p.m. yesterday to catch her picking the children up from school. I asked her to sign her permission for me to show it to other people. She agreed even though I emphasised that she could say 'No' to any of it. I mentioned how painful it must have been to watch. She remarked to the man she was with that E was crying and causing a fuss (they are my words I cannot remember her exact words). I then minimised the pain by saying I was interested in what he did next, that is, connecting.

A colleague and I had arranged to have a meeting about my PhD this morning so I took the video of E to show her, thinking it clearly showed schematic behaviour that linked to E's painful separations, that is, connecting. She began offering her interpretation (or reading of the situation). I said No to her first couple of comments because I was so convinced of what I had seen. She was suggesting that he might be interested in 'going through' rather than 'connecting'. She asked me not to close down the discussion and, all of a sudden, I became very distressed and cried. I think I was in denial about E's pain and wanting to see cognition as the soother of his pain. I said I hadn't realised how deeply his distress had affected me but of course I was crying about my own pain of separation and loss from my own children and as a child from my parents rather than E's. The pain and suffering stayed with me all day and when I got home my husband just held me and I cried.

DISCUSSION

This was the most extreme example of how my 'ghosts in the nursery' emerged, causing me to 're-enact a moment or scene from another time' (Fraiberg et al., 1987, p. 101). Fraiberg et al. (1987, p. 102) describe these ghosts as a 'repetition of the past in the present'. I was literally 'haunted' by my own early experiences of being parented and all of my energy was spent on avoiding and minimising the pain as my parents may have done with me. I was not open to any other interpretation of E's behaviour. I began to realise that even my hypothesis that schemas and emotions were connected might be a defense against pain. I began to notice what other workers said to children when children were in pain. Some could tolerate the pain and focus on the feeling, acknowledging it verbally and empathising. Others could only comfort by holding briefly and then distract. Their behaviour, like mine, may not have been within their conscious awareness.

Journal entry

Was aware when I spoke with M and A individually about the conference talk, I tried not to minimise the emotional and relational issues as I know I have a tendency to. I did however meet with A in the library and with M on the couch in the nursery, so now I am asking myself whether that was the best place for them to talk frankly to me? Was I unconsciously protecting myself from pain and conflict by meeting in a busy place?

DISCUSSION

I could not change what I had done but at least I was beginning to question my own motives. This growing awareness was certainly in my mind for the next time I met with individual parents. My awareness was growing of the need to stay with my discomfort and to allow the parents to express their feelings about their relationships with their child. I needed to think the whole scenario through each time, in advance. Next time I met with M, I went to their home but that, too, was very hectic in the evening. I need to create an emotional space for the parents to think and feel and reflect if they are to benefit from reflecting as I have been able to do.

Journal entry

Have had a very busy week training adults – am questioning my avoidance of emotions. Really difficult today when someone got upset about her father's death and then another person brought up about her husband committing suicide at 32. I ran away literally (I left the building and went towards the nursery) but then saw myself doing it – my excuse was that I wanted to ask Angela or Annette or Katey if the group could visit the nursery.

DISCUSSION

At this stage my new awareness was affecting all aspects of my life. My usual tendency was still to avoid pain, loss and separation, but, as in this case, to realise that I was avoiding emotions and to catch myself doing it so that I could behave differently.

USING LANGUAGE TO DISTANCE MYSELF FROM EMOTIONS

Journal entry

Have been writing up the well-being project for last two weeks – a mammoth task but satisfying (with four colleagues). Have never done writing in collaboration with others before. I found it an enlightening process. Keep noticing in my writing that I remove myself once from people and use objects, for example will say 'as a result of discussion it was decided' rather than 'people discussed and decided'. I am also more aware of avoiding contact with people, so will put off tasks that involve talking directly to people. Would much rather email them or even send a text. When I do that, I am not putting demands on them to respond to me and therefore I avoid being rejected.

DISCUSSION

I had begun to notice my language and to think about academic writing and the traditional notion that academic studies should be written in the third person. In fact, that was the requirement for my Master of Education study (Arnold, 1997). So this whole idea of being objective, impersonal and positivist flies in the face of acknowledging people, as actors with thoughts and feelings that affect data. Conrad (2004, p. 43) pointed out that Charles Darwin, when he wrote about his beloved daughter, Annie, who died at the age of 10, wrote very differently to his scientific papers: 'He does not use language which distances him from Annie, and does not avoid relevant emotional information about himself or Annie even if it is emotionally arousing.' I deduced that Darwin must have thought it important to include the emotional aspects of his relationship with Annie. In a similar way, I too must include emotions in a study of cognition and affect.

> ### Journal entry
>
> *Working on Methodology section – this whole issue about first or third person seems really relevant now. Chris has not given me any clear guidance but much of my writing of this section is in third but the bit I wrote on ethics is in first and it sticks out like a sore thumb, so I have been changing it. I think I need a rationale for using first sometimes, especially the section on my own awareness. Writing in the third person is like saying 'The cat did it' pretending that the study is not affected by the interests, personality or perspective of the researcher or, at least not acknowledging it. It is as though I am pretending that another person could carry out this study in exactly the same way as I did. Also at times, I find myself using language that does remove me from the equation, when it is about feelings. It's a kind of not owning up to my responsibility and feelings (Marshall, 2004).*

DISCUSSION

Shortly after this, I discarded that version of the Methodology section. I decided that writing in the first person is essential if I am writing about what I did and observed, and even my interpretation of events. What I find myself doing is slipping back into the third person as I did unconsciously a few paragraphs back (see p. 141). I left the phrase in brackets, just to illustrate my tendency to do this.

SO WHAT? THE IMPLICATIONS FOR PRACTICE

So what does all of this mean? What was the process I had been going through? What differences will my new-found knowledge of myself, and my ways of behaving, make in my practice with children and families? How can I help other workers to become more aware?

WHAT WAS THE PROCESS I HAD BEEN GOING THROUGH?

Had I allowed an element of autobiographical writing to enter what I had intended to be an academic study and was this useful? I sought support from the literature. Susan Harter (1999, p. 32) states that through language 'toddlers can now conceptualise the self as an object'. Language enables us to 'construct a "narrative" of our "life story"'. However, 'language can distort experience by creating a different (fantasised) construction of the self or by creating an unauthentic self to "meet the needs and wishes of others" (Stern)' (Harter, 1999, p. 35). Was I trying to discover a more authentic self through reflecting and writing?

Winnicott (1991) pointed out that what's going to happen may change or not, but how you feel about it and how you understand it can change through 'transitional processing'. Was the study a catalyst for change in me?

Perhaps what I was discovering is that my reflections are my truth and that is valid but may be different from another person's interpretation and will change over time as my awareness grows.

WHAT DOES THIS EVIDENCE MEAN?

Drawing on Bowlby's research, I think my 'internal working model', built up from my early interactions with others, has so far required me to be either expert or novice (1998, p. 82). I noticed near the beginning of this chapter that, at the outset, I was not able to share information with parents about emotions: 'I was happy to listen but did not want to appear critical or to offer advice to the parents.' Although I had previously felt able to conduct a dialogue with parents about cognition, when it came to emotions, I needed to feel more confident. Maybe this was because I had not been thinking about or talking about emotions with my colleagues to the extent that I was thinking and talking about cognition? It seemed risky for me to talk about concepts like 'attachment' with parents. I did not feel sufficiently confident. Perhaps I was stuck in my ways of relating, still trying to process some of the things that had happened to me?

Stern (2003, p. 97) describes 'generalized episodes', that 'contain multiple specific memories'. We build up a kind of prototype of what to expect under certain circumstances, drawn from our many experiences. These episodes contribute to the building up of an 'autobiographical memory' (Stern, 2003, p. 97). Perhaps in my family, the messages I received from those around me were that strong emotions were dangerous? This was only true of certain emotions. For a number of years I have been aware of my tendency to become excited at Christmas time and to share my bubbling excitement with others. I believe this was rooted in my early experiences within my family too, but very much focused on what was considered positive.

Stern (2003, p. 97) further describes how even preverbal infants have the ability to make 'Representations of Interactions that have been Generalized' (RIGs) and that it is from these many experiences that babies build a 'core self' (Stern, 2003, p. 99). So was I seeing myself as either expert or novice and unable or unused to risk new learning, particularly in the emotional domain?

Stern (2003, p. 115, original emphasis) points out that RIGs are different to Bowlby's 'internal working model' in the sense that RIGs are less generalised and enable us to 'activate an evoked companion', to 'reactivate an experience of I *with* another'. The raw pain I felt when viewing E's separation felt much more like an experience reactivated, than a mere model that helped me understand my generalised view of self and other.

Renk et al. (2004, p. 381) describe, from a cognitive theory perspective, 'schemas' or repeated patterns of relating to others, which they acknowledge as similar to Bowlby's internal working models and Fraiberg's ghosts in the nursery. So, was my repeated action to avoid conflict at all costs?

WHAT DIFFERENCE WILL MY NEWFOUND KNOWLEDGE AND AWARENESS MAKE IN MY PRACTICE WITH CHILDREN AND FAMILIES?

I think I am already behaving differently, although the changes are subtle. I now question more and reflect on my own actions. This reflection enables me to bring into conscious awareness my motives, which are sometimes hidden from me. For example, when I wanted the parents to decide on the video sequences for deep analysis so that any pain incurred would not be attributed to me. I was then able to see that my actions could be an avoidance of pain, rather than a promotion of an equal partnership. In this instance, I took the risk of selecting the video sequences on the basis of rich material that illustrated schemas and attachment.

I think the idea of providing 'an emotional space' for parents, that includes a quiet and uninterrupted physical space, but also a 'space in my mind' to hear what's being said is important. This applies equally to children, who sense an adult's openness to receiving painful feelings from them (Pen Green Team, 2004).

Staying with the discomfort of emotional pain and not immediately reassuring or interpreting is also important. Winnicott (1991, p. 86) described early interpretation as taking something away from a patient. It is a bit like the adult who constantly problem solves for a child and never allows them the satisfaction of solving the problem for themselves.

My greatest learning is, I think, to be able to be more aware of and to sometimes work out when I 'transfer' my feelings onto others. Drawing on the psychoanalytic literature, Shaw (1991, p. 71) defines 'transference' as 'the process whereby feelings associated with past relationships with a significant person, usually a parent, are transferred into the present situation'.

I began to experiment with this when writing the chapters on each child and sometimes found myself making an interpretation, based on my own experience, which was not necessarily like the experience of the child I was observing. For example, I judged Caitlin to feel shame and embarrassment when she misunderstood something Louise said, but, on reflection, realised that I was identifying closely with earlier experiences of my own and that I needed to look more carefully to see whether that was what Caitlin was experiencing. When I re-examined the video, there was some evidence of slight embarrassment but not to the extent that I thought I had seen initially.

HOW CAN I HELP OTHER WORKERS TO BECOME MORE AWARE?

I can share my experiences and learning with others, but that in itself will not necessarily help them to become more aware. I think it is important to share and to encourage others to study the psychoanalytic concepts that have been useful in helping me to gain greater awareness and to apply those concepts to observations they have gathered.

First-hand observation is essential. I chose to film most of the observations, so that I could reflect on them with others and over time. However, as mentioned in Chapter 1, the Tavistock method of Infant Observation involves the observer in visiting a newborn and family weekly for two years. The observation is written up afterwards and is presented as the material for a work discussion group.

Elfer (2003, 2007) has recently pioneered this way of observing for professionals working with under 3s in nursery settings. He explains that traditional observation, with the emphasis on objectivity and recording what happens without judgement, often omits the subjective feelings of the observer. However, he does caution us to be aware of whose feelings we are describing, as babies undoubtedly evoke feelings in us that may be more to do with our earlier experiences than what the baby is feeling in the here and now.

Elfer worked with a small number of Master's degree students, who were also experienced Early Years Educators, to try out his method. An important part of the process was to have regular meetings, when observation material could be shared and alternative interpretations explored.

An important part of my process was reflecting in many different ways and over time on the material gathered. The discussions with workers and parents formed the first step in that reflective process. Reading and journaling was an iterative process that stimulated my thinking and feeling. I could sometimes understand concepts through my earlier experiences more easily than I could apply them to the observations I had made. Research meetings, preparing papers and writing all enabled me to rethink and I now realise to 're-feel' the material.

In order for other workers to learn from my experiences, they would need to be open to learning from their own early experiences, as well as from their experiences of observing young children and their carers. We would need to create a context in which there was emotional space and trust for them to share and to explore the feelings evoked in them by the children they work with. A small group of five or six people could meet on a regular basis and each present material observed by them.

Elfer's group each studied up to four children over four to eight weeks. I think a great deal can be gained from a single child study (Arnold, 1999, 2003). Using video as a focus could enable the observer to share some of the detail with others and to hear what was evoked in each of the participants. Of course, using a video camera could be seen as removing oneself from the direct pain of an observation. Students at the Tavistock and Elfer's students all placed themselves in the front line, without even a notebook to distract them or to protect them from the feelings in the room.

In order to build on the work of the Pen Green Centre, I would want some of the sharing to include parents (Whalley, 2001). Perhaps, being involved in the close observation of their own child by keeping a diary of their feelings would contribute a great deal to knowledge in the field?

SUGGESTED FURTHER READING

Fonagy, P. (2001) *Attachment Theory and Psychoanalysis*, Other Press, New York.

Rustin, M. (1989) 'Encountering Primitive Anxieties' in Miller, L., Rustin, M., Rustin, M. and Shuttleworth, J. (eds) *Closely Observed Infants*, Duckworth, London.

Stern, D. (2003) *The Interpersonal World of the Infant*, Karnac Books, London.

Stern, D. (2004) *The Present Moment in Psychotherapy and Everyday Life*, W.W. Norton, London.

Conclusions and Theorising about Schemas and Emotions

Metaphors 'give form to the inexpressible'. (Lawley and Tomkins, 2000, p. 9)

This final chapter brings together:

- Some tentative generalisations about schemas and emotions

- Some emerging ideas about gender differences

- Links between schemas and metaphor, and suggests

- A concept I have named 'reflective expansion' to explain what the process might be for each child

---

INTRODUCTION

I began this part of the study with a 'hunch' that young children are motivated to explore certain schemas or repeated patterns because of emotional events in their lives at the time. This link could be made more easily with some children's actions than others. The evidence from these children is certainly not conclusive. For example, Sam was verbalising her concerns and revealing her anxieties but I could not claim that her exploration of <u>enveloping</u> was a result of her need to explore 'here and gone'. It seemed that she used that schema to explore and symbolically represent temporary and permanent absences. Similarly, Caitlin used her '<u>containing</u>' schema to surround her and her chosen play partner when she was feeling a bit low. She was already using a <u>containing</u> and <u>enveloping</u> schema in a more exploratory way when her emotional well-being was higher.

Edward seemed to be comforted by carrying out a <u>connecting</u> action shortly after a painful separation. His urge to <u>connect</u> or fix objects was very strong and enduring over time, as though he was working on something very important to him.

SOME TENTATIVE GENERALISATIONS ABOUT SCHEMAS AND EMOTIONS

Each child seemed to use schematic behaviour to represent aspects of their experiences and feelings. I thought long and hard about what those behaviours meant, the function of the repeated actions, and the motivations of the children on different occasions and over time.

THE MEANING OF THEIR ACTIONS

As I have stated earlier, we had to infer the meaning by placing the observed actions alongside information about family context. On some occasions, we were able to infer meaning in relation to a specific event, for example, when Mia started nursery, this prompted John to explore <u>going through</u> from one <u>enclosed</u> area to another repeatedly. We could make the link between a change in routine and his actions.

In other instances, the meaning of a child's explorations was less obvious and based on their emotions over a long time. For example, Susan withheld her feelings, possibly to protect her mum, and it was only towards the end of the study period that we noticed her ambivalence, which she displayed by an emphatic <u>trajectory</u> movement. '*She quite deliberately tossed the cloth containing the play people a couple of inches into the air and allowed it to drop on the floor.*' We were not able to make a direct causal link but tried to associate the behaviours with events or situations we knew about.

It seemed to us that ***their repeated actions seemed to enable each child to 'mentalise' or 'reflect' on earlier or forthcoming events*** (Fonagy, 2001, p. 176). This was particularly important when a child felt confused, for example, Cara, who was upset and confused when her granny stayed at home because her great uncle had died.

THE FUNCTION OF REPEATED ACTIONS

In a similar way to that which Segal used to define the development of symbolic play, I noticed that sometimes ***the repeated action was used as a comfort***, to return to the 'known' from something unknown or frightening (a stage at which children were possibly in denial or not understanding about a change or transition), for example when Cara 'lost herself' in playing with cornflour (Alvarez, 1996). A second *function* I thought of at first as *repair*, or beginning to act out something that might indicate that a separation could be rejoined, for example, Edward doing up door hooks or Harry tying together with string, I later thought of as ***giving form to their concern***. A third *function involved* *exploration in order to begin to understand and to accept a change/transition* (often referred to as 'working through' or 'accommodating'). Sam seemed to do this to some extent.

THE MOTIVATION TO ACT

There was little doubt that children were motivated by family events and changes to use repeated patterns in order to seek comfort, to give form to and to explore and understand emotional events. However, each child was motivated to understand events in their own way, drawing on a repertoire of repeated patterns. I never observed Sam or Caitlin <u>connecting</u> with string, even though there were changes in both families related to separation. String was freely available to all of the children in the nursery. I concluded that there was something of a gender bias towards repeatedly using certain patterns.

EMERGING IDEAS ABOUT GENDER DIFFERENCES

At first, when I reflected on each child's motivation to act, I saw from my observations that the children seemed to be engaged in

- being

- doing, or

- having (journal entry).

I subsequently added 'knowing' and 'relating' to this list. I began to think of these motives as basic psychological needs. I discovered that there was a whole body of theory on 'Self-Determination' (www.psych.rochester. edu/SDT). Within that body of theory 'basic psychological needs are assumed to be innate and universal'. According to the theory, all human beings need to feel 'competence, autonomy and relatedness' (Deci and Ryan, 2000). My earlier focus on cognition had identified the need for competence as did the children's actions. In this study, I was beginning to think about the need for relatedness.

The different schema clusters seemed to feed into the psychological needs I had identified from the data. I could see some gender differences in how frequently the individual children explored these different patterns. Ewan, Edward and John were often more focused on 'doing' by using '<u>connecting</u>', and '<u>trajectory</u>' schemas. These were the predominant patterns each boy used. Their motives seemed to be action focused. Caitlin, Sam and Susan were all interested in 'having' things and '<u>containing</u>' and '<u>transporting</u>' their things about the nursery. Sometimes 'having' was associated with 'relating'. Caitlin seemed to know the value or status of specific objects and would 'stash' new toys away in order to 'trade' or share with a friend. Sam liked to 'have' things from home. She particularly enjoyed 'having' fierce animal figures with her. They seemed to help her feel strong and fed her need to feel competent and autonomous.

The number of children studied was far too small from which to generalise about gender differences. However, when I mentioned those emerging differences to Colwyn Trevarthen, a biologist, he said that he was not surprised by the differences I had found. He referred me to the work of Hess (1954), described by Trevarthen et al. (2006). Hess suggested that:

> the animal controls its engagement with the outside world by two kinds of behaviour:
>
> (1) Active ERGOTROPIC or energy expending efforts
>
> (2) TROPHOTROPIC or energy obtaining or conserving states. (Trevarthen et al., 2006, pp. 17–18)

It seemed that, biologically, males were programmed to expend energy and females to obtain or conserve energy.

Many researchers and writers have claimed that gender is socially and culturally constructed, rather than being defined by biology alone (Harrison and Hood-Williams, 2002). We had certainly found, in an earlier study, that some girls explored 'trajectory' behaviour, but that it was less commonly displayed than in the behaviour of most boys (Arnold and Chandler, 1999). Similarly, boys displayed 'containing', 'enveloping' and 'transporting' behaviours but, again, those behaviours were not predominant in most boys. So, as far as I was concerned, the evidence was interesting but inconclusive.

I concluded that there were gender differences in this small sample that supported the findings of other small studies, but that studying a larger number of children in depth was necessary in order to discover more about gendered behaviour in relation to schemas.

LINKS BETWEEN SCHEMAS AND METAPHOR

A body of research that has supported the idea of our own actions as the basis of all of our representations and thought is the work on metaphor. Looking at metaphor from a literary perspective, Turner (1996) reported that all of literature is made up of 'image schemas' and 'action schemas' that are projected onto the stories or events that are written about in the literature. He claimed that 'EVENTS ARE ACTIONS guides us in projecting a story of action onto any kind of event-story, whether it has actors or not' (Turner, 1996, p. 38). Another 'general projection made is that ACTORS ARE MOVERS' (1996, p. 39). Whether or not the subject is a person, in literature we project our actions onto subjects and objects of action. Our own early repeated actions form the basis on which we make those projections, for example, 'she *carried* a lot of responsibility' (1996, p. 40, original emphasis) infers the '<u>transporting</u>' or carrying of something that is abstract and cannot be seen or touched.

Modell (1996, p. 219) stated that 'the locus of metaphor is now recognised to be in the mind and not in language' and that 'metaphors have their origin in the body'. He has found it unsurprising that 'affects are transformed into metaphors' as 'translating feelings into metaphors provides us with some degree of organisation and control'. Modell defined metaphor as 'the mapping of one conceptual domain onto a dissimilar conceptual domain' (Modell, 1996, p. 220). His examples related to adults rather than young children.

Modell drew on Edelman's research (Edelman and Tononi, 2000) on the brain to support his idea that 'Affects, metaphor and memory form a synergistic, unified system'. In my discussions with Chris Athey, she expressed the view that it was Edelman's research that was likely to link brain activity with schema theory. Modell informed us that,

> Edelman suggests that what is stored in the brain is not something that has a precise correspondence with the original experience, but is a potentiality awaiting activation … What is stored in memory is not a replica of the event but the potential to generalize or refind the category or class of which the event is a member. (Modell, 1996, p. 221)

This idea concurs with John Matthews's understanding and description of 'attractors' drawn from the work of Thelen and Smith (1994; Matthews, 2003). Modell claimed that 'metaphor allows us to find the familiar in the unfamiliar' and that 'memory is not only categorical but is also retranscriptive', possibly suggesting that we can come to understand or reconstruct our understanding of our earlier experiences by reflecting on them, with the benefit of increased experience (Modell, 1996, p. 221).

Chris Athey thought that the concept of 'reentry' researched by Edelman, was significant. My understanding of the link between schemas and 're-entry' is that through repetition of our actions with various materials, objects and people in different ways and across modalities, we strengthen the potential combinations of neural action.

'REFLECTIVE EXPANSION'

I was interested in making connections with Piaget's concept of 'reflective abstraction' which, he stated, was when 'certain connections are "drawn out" of the sensori-motor schemata and "projected upon" the new plane of thought' (Piaget, 1971, p. 64). In relation to Susan's understanding of her friend, Leah, going to live in Scotland, I deduced that Susan had drawn on her experiences of journeying, as a toddler and young child, to imagine or picture her friend going away (a <u>trajectory</u> movement) to a stopping-off point (Scotland). Having carried out those actions many times with her whole body, Susan could picture, in her mind, her friend going and stopping there for some time. This demonstrated how Susan, when she was developmentally ready, could draw on her earlier actions and 'abstract' from them movement and configurative aspects, to understand an event she had not experienced at first hand.

Similarly, Seymour Papert described how 'rotating circular objects against one another … carried many otherwise abstract ideas into my head' (Papert, 1980, p. vi). He explained that the action and the pattern of that action served as a model when he was faced with something new, such as, 'multiplication tables'. If he could see the tables as gears <u>rotating</u> (and he claimed he could) then he could understand how they worked. So, in effect, he was able to 'assimilate' multiplication tables into his current model of gears <u>rotating</u> against each other.

When Piaget proposed the concept of 'reflective abstraction', he did not have the benefit of brain research to support his theory. Like early childhood researchers now, he depended on what he had observed in young children's actions, representations and expressed thoughts. I believe that the concept of *reflective abstraction is viable and that young children carry forward all of their experiences in action and can draw on these to represent and think.* When Caitlin lined up several buckets and looked along the line, this heralded her later understanding of counting a line of numbers. This notion of reflective abstraction seemed to relate to the cognitive domain. The brain research seems likely to be able to explain more fully how that process occurs physiologically.

I also want to propose that there is another simultaneous process occurring which I will call *reflective expansion. When young children are faced with complex abstract concepts concerned with relationships and morality such as death and divorce, they search for connections among their earlier actions to understand and expand their knowledge.* Reflective expansion seemed to be used by children to expand their understanding of emotional events. When Sam was faced with the prospect of her parents separating, she reached back and tried to make links with the bit of that experience that she could understand and had some experience of, that is, here and gone. Sam explored '<u>enveloping</u> and revealing' in order to give form to and to begin to understand what was going to happen within her family. She also explored <u>seriation</u> in order to understand power differential and to express her worry about whether her father would survive without the rest of the family.

Rather than these processes being a kind of developmental stage theory going from less understanding to more, I would see it as more of an iterative process which could be symbolised by a dynamic circular movement going between the actions experienced and new events or experiences, with the person experiencing them at the centre.

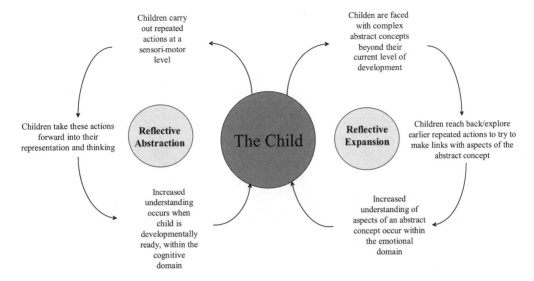

Reflective abstraction and reflective expansion occur simultaneously

Figure 10.1 Reflective abstraction and reflective expansion

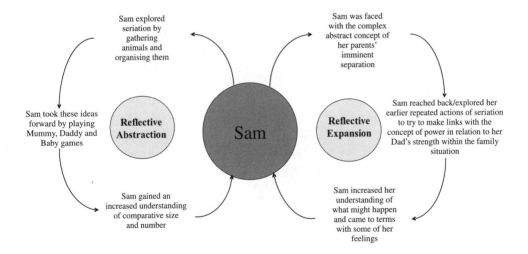

Reflective abstraction and reflective expansion occurred simultaneously

Figure 10.2 Reflective abstraction and reflective expansion: Sam

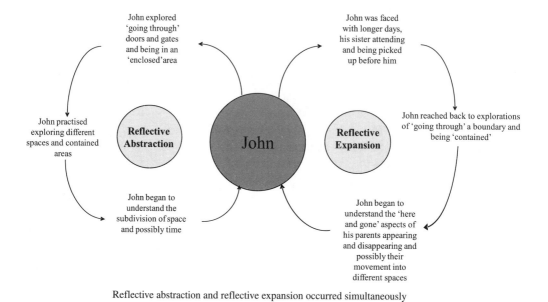

Figure 10.3 Reflective abstraction and reflective expansion: John

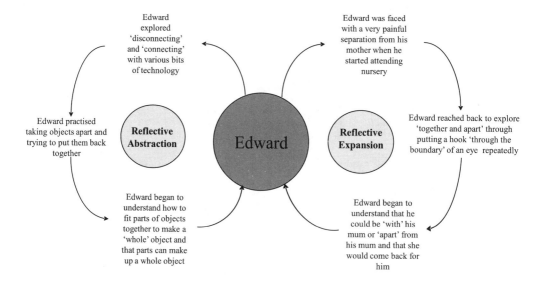

Figure 10.4 Reflective abstratction and reflective expansion: Edward

SO WHAT?

ANOTHER CONNECTION?

Late in this process of reflecting on and conceptualising the children's processes, I revisited a paper I had had for some time by Fred Levin (1997). Levin was considering 'transference' and was coming from a psychoanalytic perspective and making links with research on the brain and on cognitive development. Some of what he said resonated with me. He described 'aha' moments by stating that he had observed 'two significant basic patterns in the (brain) scanning data of Lassen, Ingvar and Skinhoj (1978)': 'First, when people are significantly interested in what they are attending to, they appear to activate simultaneously their primary cortical association areas for touch, hearing and vision; when people are engaged only half-heartedly, however, these same brain areas activate serially' (Levin, 1997, p. 1130).

This might explain why each child used patterns or schemas from their own repertoire when they were 'reaching back' to make sense of an event or information they could not understand or accept. I found myself making links with Papert's passion for <u>rotating</u> gears and with Harry's passion for string and <u>connecting</u>. When a human being is encouraged to follow their deep interests, they literally light up and the satisfaction they demonstrate is obvious to others. When children are 'deeply involved' or demonstrate 'chuffedness', they are making or have made some new connections within the affective and/or cognitive domains (Laevers, 1997; Tait, 2005). Levin also reflected on metaphor and how metaphor used in analysis could enable a patient to see a situation 'in a novel way'.

Levin saw metaphor as providing a 'bridge' between the senses, so that new insights could be made. I will continue to reflect on the function of metaphor and how it relates to schemas in young children's behaviours.

THE ROLE OF THE ADULT

Susan Isaacs was a teacher and a psychoanalyst, and was keen to differentiate between the two roles. The educator, according to Isaacs 'must be a "good" parent to the child, even though she be a strict one' (Isaacs, 1933, p. 410). The analyst needed to 'tolerate the hate and aggression' of a child, whereas the educator 'attracts to herself mainly the forces of love'. She acknowledged that her psychoanalytic training had given her insights into the children's inner worlds but she insisted that

> The psychoanalytic study of young children serves to reinforce the established values of the best practice of modern educators. The value of play,

play with companions, free imaginative play as well as play leading to ordered skill and knowledge, is enormously supported and confirmed by this deeper study of children's phantasies. (Isaacs, 1933, p. 428)

In her volume on intellectual growth, Isaacs stated that: 'They were just as free to play out their phantasies by imaginative and dramatic games as they were to garden, to cook, to sew or to go shopping' (Isaacs, 1930/1966, p. 46).

The emphasis in the Malting House School was on freedom of expression and the acceptance of and interest in the whole range of behaviours displayed by the children. Play is initiated by children, belongs to children and encapsulates their world. Play is important for infant mental health. Play is not something that can be imposed by adults or used to help children achieve outcomes decided by adults.

FINALLY

[C]onstructivists are child-centred teachers who are trying to become more conscious and more theoretically aware of what is involved in the process of 'coming to know'. Constructivists are interested in the processes by which children construct their own knowledge.
(Athey, 2007, p.43).

Young children are interested in everything around them and particularly family events. Inevitably, children are faced with separation and loss beyond their current ability to understand. Children seem to use schemas or repeated patterns of action for comfort, to give form to and to explore and begin to understand these complex life events and changes.

Bibliography

Adamo, S.M.G. (2008) Observing educational relations in their natural context, *Infant Observation*, vol. 11, no. 2, pp. 131–46.

Ainsworth, M.D.S., Blehar, M.C., Waters, E. and Wall, S. (1978) *Patterns of Attachment: A Psychological Study of the Strange Situation*, Erlbaum, Hillsdale, NJ.

Alvarez, A. (1996) The clinician's debt to Winnicott, *Journal of Child Psychotherapy*, vol. 22 no. 3, pp. 373–401.

Anthony, S. (1940) *The Child's Discovery of Death*, Routledge, London.

Arnold, C. (1990) Children who play together have similar schemas, unpublished study carried out as part of a Certificate in Post Qualifying Studies, Peterborough Regional College.

Arnold, C. (1997) Understanding young children and their contexts for learning and development: building on early experience, unpublished M.Ed. dissertation, Leicester University.

Arnold, C. (1999) *Child Development and Learning 2–5 years: Georgia's Story*, Paul Chapman, London.

Arnold, C. (2003) *Observing Harry: Child Development and Learning 0–5 years*, Open University Press, Maidenhead.

Arnold, C. (2004) The differentiated pedagogical approaches adopted by parents and workers, unpublished paper presented at the EECERA Conference, Malta, September.

Arnold, C. (2007) Young children's representations of emotions and attachment in their spontaneous patterns of behaviour: an exploration of a researcher's understanding, unpublished PhD study, Coventry University.

Arnold, C. and Chandler, T. (1999) *Gender and Schema*, unpublished conference talk presented at Pen Green Centre, Corby, Northants.

Athey, C. (1990) *Extending Thought in Young Children*, Paul Chapman, London.

Athey, C. (2003) Personal communication.

Athey, C. (2007) *Extending Thought in Young Children*, 2nd edn, Paul Chapman, London.

Bartholomew, L. and Bruce, T. (1993) *Getting to Know You: A Guide to Record-keeping in Early Childhood Education and Care*, Hodder and Stoughton, London.

Berlin, L.J. and Cassidy, J. (1999) Relations among relationships, in J. Cassidy and P. Shaver (eds), *Handbook of Attachment: Theory, Research and Clinical Applications*, Guilford Press, New York.

Bettelheim, B. (1956/1990) *Recollections and Reflections*, Thames and Hudson, London.

Bion, W. (1962) *Learning Through Experience*, Heinemann, London.

Bowlby, J. (1997) *Attachment and Loss Volume 1*, Pimlico, London.

Bowlby, J. (1998) *Attachment and Loss Volume 2*, Pimlico, London.

Bruce, T. (1991) *Time to Play in Early Childhood Education*, Hodder and Stoughton, London.

Bruce, T. (2001) *Learning Through Play*, Hodder and Stoughton, London.

Bruce, T. (2004) *Developing Learning in Early Childhood*, Paul Chapman, London.

Carr, M. (2001) *Assessment in Early Childhood Settings: Learning Stories*, Paul Chapman, London.

Cassidy, J. (1999) The nature of the child's ties, in J. Cassidy and P.R. Shaver (eds), *Handbook of Attachment: Theory, Research and Clinical Applications*, Guilford Press, New York.

Cassidy, J. and Shaver, P.R. (1999) *Handbook of Attachment: Theory, Research and Clinical Applications*, Guilford Press, New York.

Conrad, R. (2004) '(A)s if She Defied the World in her Joyousness': rereading Darwin on emotion and emotional development, *Human Development*, vol. 47, pp. 40–65.

Copley, B. and Forryan, B. (1987) *Therapeutic Work with Children and Young People*, Cassell, Trowbridge.

Corsaro, W.A. (2003) *We're Friends Right? Inside Kids' Culture*, Joseph Henry Press, Washington, DC.

Damasio, A. (1999) *The Feeling of What Happens*, Harvest Books, New York.

Deci, E.L. and Ryan, R.M. (2000) The 'what' and 'why' of goal pursuits: Human needs and the self-determination of behaviour, *Psychological Inquiry*, vol. 11, pp. 227–68.

Easen, P., Kendall, P. and Shaw, J. (1992) Parents and educators: dialogue and development through partnership, *Children and Society*, vol. 6, no. 4, pp. 282–96.

Edelman, G.M. and Tononi, G. (2000) *A Universe of Consciousness*, Basic Books, New York.

Elfer, P. (1996) Building intimacy in relationships with young children in nurseries, *Early Years*, vol. 16, no. 2, pp. 30–4.

Elfer, P. (2003) Observation observed, draft chapter for book entitled *Birth–Three Matters*, Open University Press, Maidenhead.

Elfer, P. (2007) Babies and young children in nurseries: using psychoanalytic ideas to explore tasks and interactions, *Children and Society*, vol. 21, no. 2, pp. 111–22.

Elfer, P. and Dearnley, K. (2007) Nurseries and emotional well-being: evaluating an emotionally containing model of professional development, *Early Years*, vol. 27, no. 3, pp. 267–79.

Elfer, P. and Dearnley, K. (2008) Symposium at EECERA Conference, Stavanger, September.

Ellis, C. and Bochner, A.P. (2000) Autoethnography, personal narrative, reflexivity: researcher as subject, in N.K. Denzin and Y.S. Lincoln (eds), *Handbook of Qualitative Research*, Sage, London.

Fawcett, M. (1996) *Learning Through Child Observation*, Jessica Kingsley, London.

Fletcher, C. (2006) Personal communication.

Fonagy, P. (1999) Psychoanalytic theory from the viewpoint of attachment theory and research, in J. Cassidy and P.R. Shaver (eds), *Handbook of Attachment*, Guilford Press, London.

Fonagy, P. (2001) *Attachment Theory and Psychoanalysis*, Other Press, New York.

Formosinho, J. (2003) Personal communication.

Fraiberg, S.H., with Adelson, E. and Shapiro, V. (1987) Ghosts in the nursery: a psychoanalytic approach to the problem of impaired infant-mother relationships, in L. Fraiberg (ed.), *Selected Writings of Selma Fraiberg*, Ohio State University, Columbus, OH.

Gopnik, A., Meltzoff, A. and Kuhl, P. (1999) *How Babies Think*, Weidenfeld and Nicolson, London.

Hare, J., Sugawara, A. and Pratt, C. (1986) The child in grief: implications for teaching, *Early Child Development and Care*, vol. 25, pp. 43–56.

Harrison, W.C. and Hood-Williams, J. (2002) *Beyond Sex and Gender*, Sage Publications, London.

Harter, S. (1999) *The Construction of Self*, Guilford Press, New York.

Hess, W.R. (1954) *Diencephalon: Autonomic and Extrapyramidal Funcyions*, Grune and Stratton, Orlando, FL, in Trevarthen, C., Aitken, K,J., Vandekerckhove, M., Delafield-Butt, J. and Nagy, E. (2006) Collaborative regulations of vitality in early childhood: stress in intimate relationships and postnatal psychopathology, in D. Cicchetti and D.J. Cohen (eds), *Developmental Psychopathology*, 2nd edn, Wileys, New York.

Hobson, P. (2002) *The Cradle of Thought*, Macmillan, London.

Holmes, J. (1993) *John Bowlby and Attachment Theory*, Routledge, London.

Hopkins, J. (1988) Facilitating the development of intimacy between nurses and infants in day nurseries, *Early Child Development and Care*, vol. 33, pp. 99–111.

Isaacs, S. (1930/1966) *Intellectual Growth in Young Children*, Routledge and Kegan Paul, London.

Isaacs, S. (1933) *Social Development in Young Children*, George Routledge and Sons, London.

Isaacs, S. (1952) The nature and function of phantasy, in J. Riviere (ed.), *Developments in Psychoanalysis*, Hogarth Press, London.

Jackson, E. (2004) Trauma revisited: a 5-year-old's journey from experiences, to thoughts, to words, towards hope, *Journal of Child Psychotherapy*, vol. 30, no. 1, pp. 53–70.

Janesick, V. (2000) The choreography of qualitative research design, in N.K. Denzin and Y.S.Lincoln (eds), *Handbook of Qualitative Research*, Sage, London.

Johnson, H. (1972) *Children in 'The Nursery School'*, Agathon Press, New York. First published 1928.

Jordan, B. and Henderson, A. (1995) 'Interaction analysis: foundations and practice', *The Journal of the Learning Sciences*, vol. 4, no. 1, pp. 39–103.

Jordan, R. and Powell, S. (1995) *Understanding and Teaching Children with*

Autism, Wiley, New York.

Kraemer, S. (2000) Promoting resilience: changing concepts of parenting and child care, conference talk at the Pen Green Centre, Corby, Northants, March.

Laevers, F. (1997) *A Process-Oriented Child Follow-up System for Young Children*, Centre for Experiential Education, Leuven University, Belgium.

Lawley, J. and Tomkins, P. (2000) *Metaphors in Mind*, The Developing Company Press, London.

Levin, F.M. (1997) Integrating some mind and brain views of transference: the phenomena, *Journal of the American Psychoanalytic Association*, vol. 45, no. 4, pp. 1121–51.

Marrone, M. with Diamond, N. (1998) *Attachment and Interaction*, Jessica Kingsley Publishers, London.

Marshall, J. (2004) Living systemic thinking: exploring quality in first-person action research, *Action Research*, vol 2, no. 3, pp. 309–29.

Matthews, J. (2003) *Drawing and Painting: Children and Visual Representation*, Paul Chapman, London.

Meade, A. and Cubey, P. (2008) *Thinking Children: Learning About Schemas*, Open University Press, Maidenhead.

Michel, J.M and Arnold, C. (2005) 'Sharing perspectives over Jordan', conference talk at Pen Green Research Base, April.

Miller, L., Rustin, M., Rustin, M. and Shuttleworth, J. (eds) (1989) *Closely Observed Infants*, Duckworth, London.

Modell, A.H. (1996) Reflections on metaphor and affects, paper presented to the Chicago Psychoanalytic Society, 28 May.

Music, G. (2004) The old one-two, *Journal of Child Psychotherapy*, vol. 30, no. 1, pp. 21–37.

Nutbrown, C. (2006) *Threads of Thinking*, 3rd edn, Sage, London.

Papert, S. (1980) *Mindstorms*, Harvester Press, Brighton.

Pen Green Team (2004) A research and development project to promote well-being and resilience in young children, unpublished study, Pen Green Centre, Corby, Northants.

Piaget, J. (1950/2001) *The Psychology of Intelligence*, Routledge, London.

Piaget, J. (1951) *Play, Dreams and Imitation in Childhood*, William Heinemann, London.

Piaget, J. (1962) *Les relations entre l'affectivite et l'intelligence dans le developpe-*

ment mental de l'enfant, C.D.U., Paris.

Piaget, J. (1971) *Structuralism*, Routledge and Kegan Paul, London.

Piaget, J. and Inhelder, B. (1956) *The Child's Conception of Space*, Routledge and Kegan Paul, London.

Piaget, J. and Inhelder, B. (1969) *The Psychology of the Child*, Routledge and Kegan Paul, London.

Podmore, V.N. (2006) *Observation*, NZCER Press, Wellington.

Prodger, A. (2005) Susan's containing schema, conference talk, Pen Green Centre, Corby, Northants.

Reay, D. (2002) Gendering Bourdieu's concept of capitals? emotional capital, women and social class, paper presented at the Feminists Evaluate Bourdieu Conference, Manchester University, 11 October.

Renk, K., Roddenberry, A. and Oliveros, A. (2004) 'A cognitive reframing of ghosts in the nursery', *Journal of Child and Family Studies*, vol. 13, no. 4, pp. 377–84.

Rinaldi, C. (2006) *In Dialogue with Reggio Emilia: Listening, Researching and Learning*, Routledge, London.

Rodier, P.M. (2000) The early origins of autism, *Scientific American*, February, pp. 38–45.

Rustin, M. (1989) 'Encountering Primitive Anxieties', in Miller, L., Rustin, M., Rustin, M. and Shuttleworth, J. (eds), *Closely Observed Infants*, Duckworth, London.

Shaw, J. (1991) An investigation of parents' conceptual development in the context of dialogue with a community teacher, unpublished PhD, Newcastle University.

Shaw, J. (2005) Personal communication during a seminar at Pen Green Research Base, Corby, Northants.

Shuttleworth, J. (1994) Dealing with Distress, pp. 305–6, in J. Oates (ed.), *The Foundations of Child Development*, Open University, Milton Keynes.

Soale, V. (2004) What's going on inside John's head? unpublished dissertation as part of a Master's degree in Early Childhood Education with Care, London Metropolitan University.

Solomon, J. and George, C. (1999) The measurement of attachment security in infancy and childhood, in J. Cassidy and P.R. Shaver (eds), *Handbook of Attachment: Theory, Research and Clinical Applications*, Guilford Press, New York.

Stern, D. (1998) *The Motherhood Constellation*, Karnac, London.

Stern , D. (2003) *The Interpersonal World of the Infant*, Karnac Books, London.

Stern, D. (2004) *The Present Moment in Psychotherapy and Everyday Life*, W.W. Norton, London.

Tait, C. (2004) 'Chuffedness', unpublished paper presented at the EECERA Conference, Malta, September.

Tait, C. (2005) Chuffedness as an indicator of good quality in an infant and toddler nest, paper presented at the EECERA Conference, Dublin, September.

Tait, C. (2007) Thinking about feeling: facilitating reflection, unpublished dissertation submitted as part of a Master's degree in Integrated Provision for Children and Families, University of Leicester.

Thelen, E. and Smith, L.B. (1994) *A Dynamic Systems Approach to the Development of Cognition and Action*, MIT Press, Cambridge, MA.

Tobin, J. and Davidson, D. (1990) The ethics of polyvocal ethnography: empowering vs. textualizing children and teachers, *Qualitative Studies in Education*, vol. 3, no. 3, pp. 271–83.

Trevarthen, C. (2002) Learning in companionship, *Education in the North: The Journal of Scottish Education*, New Series, no. 10, pp. 16–25.

Trevarthen, C. (2003) Chuffedness – the motor of learning, Pen Green Conference, June.

Trevarthen (2006) Personal communication.

Trevarthen, C. and Aitken, K.J. (2001) Infant intersubjectivity: research, theory and clinical applications, *Journal of Child Psychology Psychiatry*, vol. 42, no. 1, pp. 3–48.

Trevarthen, C., Aitken, K.J., Vandekerckhove, M., Delafield-Butt, J. and Nagy, E. (2006) Collaborative regulations of vitality in early childhood: stress in intimate relationships and postnatal psychopathology, in D. Cicchetti and D.J. Cohen (eds), *Developmental Psychopathology*, 2nd edn, Wileys, New York.

Turner, M. (1996) *The Literary Mind*, Oxford University Press, Oxford.

Vygotsky, L.S. (1978) *Mind in Society*, Harvard University Press, London.

Whalley, M. (ed.) (1997) *Working with Parents*, Hodder and Stoughton, Sevenoaks.

Whalley, M. (ed.) (2001) *Involving Parents in their Children's Learning*, Paul Chapman, London.

Whalley, M. (ed.) (2007) *Involving Parents in their Children's Learning*, 2nd edn, Paul Chapman, London.

Whalley, M. (2009) Personal communication.

Whalley, M. and Arnold, C. (1997) Parental involvement in education, summary of findings for Teacher Training Agency.

Wickes, F.G. (1978) *The Inner World of Childhood*, Sigo Press, Boston, MA. First published in 1927.

Winnicott, D.W. (1975) *Through Paediatrics to Psychoanalysis: Collected Papers*, Karnac Books, London.

Winnicott, D.W. (1965/1990) *The Maturational Processes and the Facilitating Environment*, Karnac Books, London.

Winnicott, D.W. (1991) *Playing and Reality*, Brunner-Routledge, Hove.

Winnicott, D.W. (2006) *The Family and Individual Development*, Routledge Classic, London. First published 1965.

Wittenberg, I. (1999) *The Emotional Experience of Teaching and Learning*, Karnac, London.

Yirmiya, N. and Sigman, M (2001) Attachment in children with autism, in J. Richer and S. Coates (eds), *Autism – The Search for Coherence*, Jessica Kingsley, London.

Index

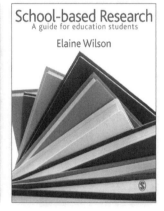

Supporting researchers for more than forty years

Research methods have always been at the core of SAGE's publishing. Sara Miller McCune founded SAGE in 1965 and soon after, she published SAGE's first methods book, *Public Policy Evaluation*. A few years later, she launched the Quantitative Applications in the Social Sciences series – affectionately known as the 'little green books'.

Always at the forefront of developing and supporting new approaches in methods, SAGE published early groundbreaking texts and journals in the fields of qualitative methods and evaluation.

Today, more than forty years and two million little green books later, SAGE continues to push the boundaries with a growing list of more than 1,200 research methods books, journals, and reference works across the social, behavioural, and health sciences.

From qualitative, quantitative and mixed methods to evaluation, SAGE is the essential resource for academics and practitioners looking for the latest in methods by leading scholars.

www.sagepublications.com